WAREHOUSE
VETERAN

Your Tactical Field Guide to Industrial Real Estate

John B. Jackson, CCIM

Editor and Project Management: Front Rowe Seat Communications, karen@karenrowe.com

Printed in the United States of America
FIRST EDITION
Library of Congress
ISBN: 978-0-9973298-0-3

Library of Congress CIP Pending

Published by INDCRE Publishing

I dedicate this book to our fallen heroes,

the men and women of the United States military,

who have fought bravely for our freedom

and have paid the ultimate sacrifice.

Table of Contents

Foreword

Lee E Arnold JR. CCIM CRE

Executive Chairman Colliers International FL

I know what you're thinking -- who writes a book about buying, sell-ing and leasing warehouses specifically for business owners? It takes a driven professional with a diverse skillset. John B. Jackson definitely has the discipline and has invested the time to meet this formidable author challenge. I know John through our work together at Colliers Interna-tional Florida. He has a robust background in commercial real estate, finance, construction, and development. He has designed, constructed purchased, sold and leased warehouses. When it comes to industrial facilities, he is an expert.

As the Founder, Chairman of the Board and CEO of the Arnold Com-panies a consortium of businesses including: Colliers International — Central Florida Markets, L.A. Financial, and Clearwater Bay Associates I have seen billions of dollars of complex transactions. Collectively, for over 43 years, these companies have provided commercial investment brokerage, property management, valuation, development, and capital market services.

My commercial real estate experience is centered around a specialization in large, one-of-a-kind marketing assignments with an emphasis on problem properties. I can tell you the commercial investment real estate landscape is complicated. There are risks to consider when acquiring or leasing industrial real estate. Even property development requires a full understanding of the process and how to analyze all the options. The purpose of each project drives effective strategies. Defining the purpose from the beginning is as important as the execution and follow through.

While there have been several guides written about real estate acquisition strategy, generally they are directed at the investor. *Warehouse Veteran: Your Tactical Field Guide to Industrial Real Estate* is written for the user of the space and specifically the business owner. John's disciplined approach takes you through the technical aspects of the process with detail and precision. As you read this book, think of it as a reference manual designed to provide an overview of the most important aspects to consider when making commercial real estate decisions. It serves as a primer to save you time, avoid problems and produce better outcomes. The book will assist you to make key real estate decisions based on your company's goals by leveraging critical hidden market knowledge and following proven processes. More importantly, you will be armed with the tools and knowledge necessary to avoid many serious pitfalls that could negatively impact your company's bottom line.

Furthermore, I would like to acknowledge and commend John who is donating 100% of the proceeds from this book to support wounded veterans' charitable causes. I personally know how important it is for John to give back to the wounded veterans.

Every transaction is different, but using the right advisor on your team can mean the difference between a disappointing loss and a successful outcome.

A Note to Readers

Broker Versus Advisor

Throughout this book, I will use the term real estate broker and real estate advisor interchangeably, but to clearly define the difference, a real estate broker accurately describes, at a summary level, what we do and is a recognizable term in the industry. It also implies that the broker is licensed and is a conduit to the real estate transaction.

Specifically, as a real estate advisor, I view my role from a consultative approach, working with clients to think through all the possibilities and alternatives, analyze their options, and help them make the best decision for their particular circumstance and situation.

Introduction

Strategy without tactics is the slowest route to victory.

Tactics without strategy is the noise before defeat. – SUN TZU

Kaboom! The dead silence of night erupts into a crescendo of fireworks across the pitch-black sky. We grab our chemical protection gear, our rifles and equipment, and race out into the night. My heart pumps as I see the scores of A-10 Wart Hog (tank killer) planes flying overhead in formation, one after another.

It is 0230 hours on 17 January, 1991. I just retired to my dusty green army cot for some badly needed rest after a four-hour perimeter guard shift around our forward operating base in Northern Saudi Arabia. We have been parked in this spot for over a month now, digging in and waiting with the 3rd Armored Division as a part of Operation Desert Shield.

Now our unit is awake and alert, fully engaged in Operation Desert Storm. We move forward with the Division into Kuwait City over the next 24 hours and remain in Kuwait and Iraq for a number of months following the invasion. The campaign is a striking success, due to a number of factors including technological advantage, exceptional intel, superior logistics and supply chain capabilities, training and preparation, and force dominance.

While we were wildly successful in the grand scheme, conditions were challenging on a personal level. I think we went thirty-six days without a shower. Lack of sleep was compounded by the ever-present threat of missiles, possibly carrying chemical agents. Although we had vaccines and chemical suits, we lived in daily fear that Saddam Hussein might launch a chemical agent attack on us. The experience is one I will most certainly never forget, and one that changed me forever.

> "Success is best achieved when you reach the point in which preparation meets opportunity."

Even now, almost 25 years later, the takeaways and lessons are still as clear as they were then. Success is best achieved when you reach that point in which preparation meets opportunity. Thoughtful strategic planning, followed with systematic execution, produces superior results. This applies to wartime, peacetime, and even business. My business is commercial real estate. Specifically, I specialize in industrial facilities ranging in size from 20,000 square foot stand-alone buildings to industrial parks including hundreds of thousands of square feet of inventory.

While you may not be woken up by artillery in your daily life at 0230 in the morning, it's possible that you experience some anxiety and an occasional sleepless night related to your business and facility needs. When it comes to buying, selling, developing, and leasing industrial real estate, strategic planning, effective preparation, and consistent follow-thru significantly increase the probability of a successful outcome in your favor. I wrote this book to bring awareness to proven processes and procedures that will assist you with the strategic planning and effective preparation you need to succeed.

Most businesses have facility needs. The content in this book is directed toward the business owner who requires warehouse, distribution, manufacturing, or flex space to operate a business. Business owners will encounter many different facility-related decision points during the course of their careers and, in this book, I choose to focus on two scenarios:

The first is the business with changing facility needs. This could be due to an upcoming lease expiration, a business expansion, a contraction, or some strategic shift, such as a geographic realignment or a change in production methods, that forces a change in the facility type or location. In that situation, the owner has a decision to make: Do I lease or own? If I own, do I buy existing or develop my own, or should I consider a combination of these?

The second scenario I focus on in Warehouse Veteran is that of a business owner or investor whose property doesn't necessarily require a change in configuration for business reasons. Perhaps the owner is contemplating retirement, or a change in lifestyle or business. Here again, a decision must be made regarding whether to sell the facility, hold it, or do a sale-leaseback, something I'll explain in detail in a later chapter.

As we go further into the book, we'll examine all the different considerations that apply to these scenarios, and I will provide you with a primer on each of the related topics. Written as a field guide, this book allows the reader to pick it up and turn to a specific chapter to access information on specific transaction related topics like: site selection factors, lease versus own analysis, and the acquisition process. At its highest level, this book is structured to mirror the life cycle of a real estate transaction, starting with the primary components of acquisition and moving through disposition. The framework of the content is best visualized with the following graphic:

The key to success, when it comes to facility-related business situations, is effective strategic analysis and tactical execution. One thing I see a lot of in the market is business owners and managers taking on the burden of managing their own commercial real estate needs in addition to running their core businesses. In 99 percent of the cases, they are putting their businesses, and sometimes their personal wealth, at a disadvantage. It could be that they don't have the proper commercial real estate training and experience, or maybe they are simply too busy to focus on the tactical and methodical planning and execution of a complex real estate deal.

For example, let's take a company that just won a large five year production contract and needs to increase output, the big question is how to handle the increased production requirement. Should an additional facility be leased or a new larger property be purchased or developed? If, through strategic analysis, the business determines that the best course of action is to lease an additional facility, then a specific process should be followed in order to optimize the outcome. If the best option is to own, then the question is whether to acquire an existing facility or develop one from the ground up.

If you buy an existing property, a specific process should be followed, which I cover in Chapter Eight. If you decide to develop your own facility or lease a build-to-suit, specific questions should be explored and processes should be followed. I cover important information about development-related topics in Chapter Ten.

In *Warehouse Veteran*, I'll take you through a series of decision-making processes that apply to each of the different components of acquisition and disposition of industrial facilities. It's a complicated landscape, one requiring an experienced guide with the skillset and tools to get you through the terrain unharmed, as well as to help develop a pathway leading to the best outcome for you and your business while offering the least amount of risk.

This book is for you if you are considering making a very important commercial real estate investment and you want to understand the critical concepts necessary to optimize the outcome of your transaction.

This book is for you if you have already bought, sold, or leased commercial real estate, and you understand that we operate in a complex market that requires skillful planning with precision execution in order to succeed.

This book is also for you if you're going to build a facility for your business, and if you're considering purchasing land for development and could benefit from a primer on the site selection process.

I've seen too many people make costly mistakes, and the purpose of this field guide is to help you avoid those mistakes. It is a primer on key topics that can make or break your success in a commercial real estate transaction. It will provide you with a framework and arm you with the processes and knowledge you need to make good decisions in your future.

Successful commercial real estate transactions begin with good analysis and planning, and they end well with successful execution. Each transaction should be viewed as a process with multiple steps, checks, and balances throughout. Failure to consider all the pitfalls or explore all the options could lead to disaster. My goal is to help you to understand and consider the possibilities before you make critical decisions that will impact your business and your life.

Chapter 1:
Riding the Wave of Change

"It is not the strongest or the most intelligent who will survive but those who can best manage change." - CHARLES DARWIN

The vast amount of information shared each day through our globally connected network is driving major change in supply chains and the way we move goods and products into our homes and businesses.

Increasingly, we look for ways to separate from the pack, and we are aware that every decision can have major impact on our business.

It is natural to become complacent when things are working —"If it ain't broke, don't fix it" — but there are pitfalls in this clichéd form of thought. The old mentality of being resistant to change is what gets us into trouble as our world continues to advance at an increasing rate.

The analogy we used to hear in business school was the plight of the 13,000 buggy whip business- es thriving in the 1890's before

automobiles were introduced into the market. The buggy whip manu-facturers didn't accommodate change, and where are they now?

Industry specific evolution due to disruptive factors has always oc-curred, but the pace at which it is occurring is rapidly increasing. What taxi company in 2011 would have guessed the effect that Uber could potentially have on their industry and their businesses?

Look at the effect of iTunes on the music industry, or Amazon on traditional retail models. Sometimes the change is gradual, and some-times it seems to occur overnight.

Real estate is not immune to change. For the residential broker, information that was once proprietary and guarded on the MLS is now available to anyone with a smartphone and a data plan.

Commercial real estate is also not immune to rapid change and is driven by new technologies. Although available information on com-mercial properties is still somewhat limited, a channel does exist for buyers and sellers to connect on some level via various sites like Loo-pNet, Showcase, and Craigslist. What is missing in these sites are the important details in the background, access to all available options, the comparative analysis, the influence of experience and insight, and most importantly, the execution and follow-through on research and due diligence that a website simply cannot provide.

Perhaps one day, commercial real estate will evolve to a point where users and owners are connected in a truly efficient market, but I can tell you that it will not happen in this decade. Buyers and sellers, landlords and tenants, owners and contractors have always had some conflict of interest, each desiring the best outcome for his own situation. Regardless of which side of the transaction you happen to reside on, there is no substitute for having all available information, developing a strategic plan that bests suits your interests, and executing on that plan. Surrounding yourself with the right advisors is the direct pathway to maximizing the outcome in your favor.

Good Help is Hard to Find

In *The Wealth of Nations*, Adam Smith wrote about the basic factors required for economic production as being land (real estate), labor, and capital. As our population continues to grow, we need additional places to work, sleep, eat, shop, and live. Throughout history, the supply of buildings to meet these needs has fluctuated, with too little space available during times of rapid growth, and oversupply when growth slows. The delay between growth of demand and eventual response in supply is the main driver that causes the volatility we experience in real estate market cycles.

Industrial real estate is no exception, and it is largely cyclical by nature. Warehouse, distribution, and manufacturing space supply-and-demand will continue to ebb and flow into the future. Many macro-economic factors contribute to changing values. The macro business climate, shifts in supply chain, interest rates, supply and demand of existing facilities, and geo-political factors can all contribute to the cycles for certain types of commercial properties.

One of the biggest challenges owners and users of commercial real estate face today is harnessing the complexity and pitfalls that each potential scenario presents. Chances are, there are multiple options to analyze for any given situation, and overlooking even one of those options could cost the business owner hundreds of thousands—and in some cases, millions—in potential wealth.

Unfortunately, when it comes to commercial brokers and advisors, there tends to be a fire-and-forget mentality in the business, especially when the market is improving and things are hot. In my experience as an owner, developer, landlord, and tenant, it is critical to seek out and work with thorough, methodical, loyal, and driven professionals. The best outcomes are derived when your internal team and industrial real estate advisor work through tactical planning and execution, as well as identifying and mitigating all potential risks throughout the various stages.

Define your requirement and then seek out a commercial real estate advisor that specializes in your specific transaction type. For example, if you are a Craft Brewing Company, seek out a broker with a track record of representing Craft Breweries, as they have specific facility requirements that, left out of your acquisition criteria, could cost you big down the road if you have to retrofit an inadequate facility. If you are considering a 1031 exchange or a sale leaseback, or perhaps just want to compare the potential financial outcome of disposing of your facility versus holding and leasing out over the next ten years, make sure to interview brokers with proven financial analysis skills.

Beyond experience, other character related factors should be identified and sought out. Working with brokers with an outstanding track record for performance, integrity, and superior communication skills is critical. You wouldn't trust a surgeon with less than average performance stats and ratings to operate on you, so why would you work with a broker who is less than top-notch?

Chapter 2:
Evolve and Prosper

"Things work out best for those who make the best of how things work out." - JOHN WOODEN

"Sorry, John, but the seventeen-million-dollar project you were just awarded has been put on hold."

It is 2006, the very beginning of the housing industry's recognition that we are heading into a period of major economic disruption.

"It's a corporate decision. All new projects that haven't yet started are now being put on hold."

I can hear the words, but I am speechless. A knot grows in the pit of my stomach and, throat closed, mouth dry, I wonder what will come next.

The man delivering the news is a national developer of residential subdivisions and one of my biggest clients. I have just ramped up my crews and equipment, in preparation for this job, and putting this project on hold will present a major challenge to the future profitability of my business.

We adapt and immediately start bidding more aggressively on other commercial development projects, but the writing is on the wall. The market seems to implode almost overnight, and it's time to adjust the business model in order to avoid a crash landing. Of course, we soon learned that all of our competitors were also doing the same thing. The industry was consolidating and margins were shrinking.

My management team analyzed courses of action and determined that the best thing to do was reduce reliance on heavy equipment, offload the overhead, seek out limited competition opportunities with clients that had the financial strength to pay, and adapt the business model to accommodate these new changes in the market.

After lots of research and consulting trusted advisors, the solution became clear. We finished the development projects we were committed to in the underground utility site work business, then began to change our focus.

The next step in my business evolution included specializing in federal construction and development projects as a general contractor, helping fellow veterans by restoring, repurposing, and building additions at Department of Veterans' Affairs Hospitals throughout Florida and Georgia.

Although we'd stopped working with privately funded clients and were pursuing projects with the federal government, we used the same business methodology. I wrote my business plan, made changes based on external feedback, sought out the most talented team I could find, and built a new thriving business. Within two years, we were working in eight different hospitals and producing $20 million in annual revenue with very healthy margins.

By winning long-term contracts called Multiple Award Task Order Contracts (MATOCs), which are limited competition contracts, my company became a logical and attractive target for other similar businesses doing the same type of work in different regions.

MATOCs are bundled contracts to cover construction projects for a specific facility or geographic region. They are typically five years in duration, and if you're not an awardee of the MATOC, you're not going to get any of the hundreds of millions of dollars in task orders awarded during the life of the MATOC contract. As an awardee of five separate MATOCs, my design build construction management company became actively pursued by other companies, and was eventually bought out by a regional competitor at the end of 2013.

Next Step in Evolution

For those of you who have sold a company, you already know that you can only stay on vacation for a limited period of time before going absolutely insane with boredom. After several lengthy fishing and diving trips in remote places around the world, I realized it was time to get back to work.

The goal for my next career evolution was to bring together the culmination of my development and construction experience, financial analysis capabilities, commercial real estate experience, and love for working with people in different businesses and situations. This led me the job of commercial real estate advisor at Colliers International (Ticker: CIGI), specializing in the sale, purchase, leasing, and development of industrial properties.

I am a founding member of one of the top industrial teams in our market. At Colliers, I do more than represent clients and advise others through publications, blogs, and videos at our team website, TampaBayIndustrialAdvisors.com. I also own several commercial real estate assets as an investor and personally manage them myself.

I have been a buyer, seller, landlord, tenant, and a developer of multiple commercial real estate properties over the years. I've developed infrastructure, which is what happens beneath the development. I've developed the buildings—the vertical component of a project. I've owned them, marketed them, leased them, and sold them. In other words, I'm an expert in all aspects of the various transactions surrounding these buildings that my clients purchase, develop, and occupy. I've been a part of the process from every perspective.

And that is why I have written Warehouse Veteran. I hope to share my diverse yet related experience in order to provide benefit to others, and I want to help them avoid the pitfalls, benefit from the lessons learned, and profit in every commercial real estate situation possible.

Taking Care of the Troops

As a former Army Officer and Desert Storm Veteran, I owe a great deal of gratitude to the military and the veterans that protect our freedom both at home and abroad. I have countless stories and examples of how military training and experience benefitted my life and the lives of others as they transitioned from military service into private sector industries.

As with most Americans, I have a strong passion for standing behind those who serve and supporting our troops in every way that I can. And for me, it's more than donating money. It's about bringing awareness to our friends and neighbors, making them aware of the plight of our Wounded Warriors. It's about volunteering time and resources to assist those in need.

In keeping with this approach and dedication to supporting our heroes, I have committed to donating 100 percent of the proceeds from this book to veteran related causes such as the Intrepid Fallen Heroes Fund, Paws for Patriots, and the Fisher House Foundation. Every dollar you and others spend on purchasing this book and all related materials will go directly to fund veterans' charitable organizations.

Chapter 3:
Timing Is Everything
– A Primer On Market Cycles

"You don't have to swing hard to hit a home run.
If you've got the timing, it'll go." – YOGI BERRA

While we have all heard that the first rule in real estate is "location, location, location," and I acknowledge its importance, I also believe that it is just as important to consider "timing, timing, timing." Determining the best time to buy and sell for your specific situation depends on a multitude of factors, many of which are related to your specific industry and your unique personal and business requirements. Market cycles should always be considered in that equation because timing can mean the difference between making and losing millions.

The best case scenario for acquisition, disposition, and leasing is to understand and use market condition awareness in your favor by taking a strategic approach to timing your transactions, understanding where we currently are in the market cycle, and how that will potentially affect the outcome of the transaction. Also, integrating a market cycle analysis into your long-term strategy can significantly affect your wealth. While changes in your business may drive you into a scenario where you have no choice but to buy, sell, or lease, at a specific point in time, it is still important to understand how current market cycle conditions will affect your situation.

To help decode the process for you, I have summarized the most common characteristics of the four distinct phases of the commercial real estate cycle: Recovery, Expansion, Hypersupply and Recession.

Market Cycle Quadrants*

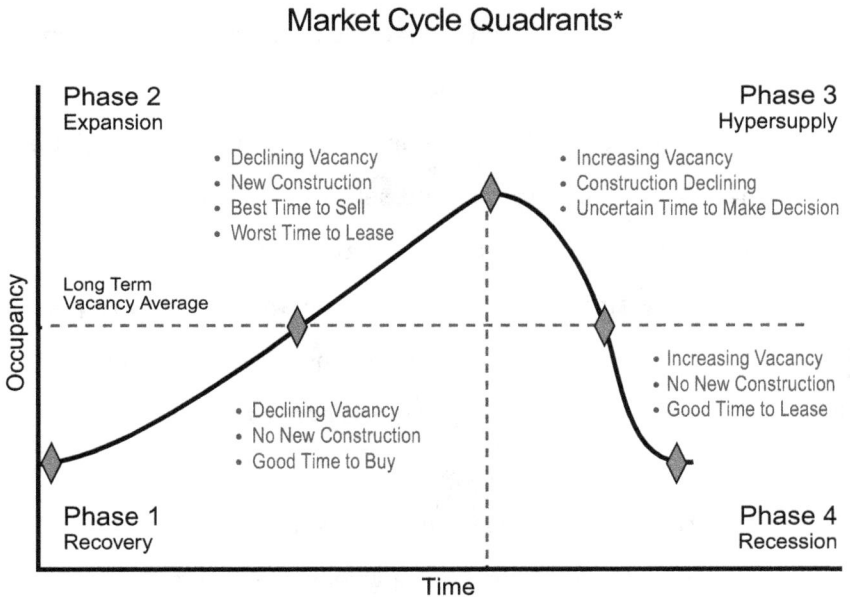

* Graph modified from original by Glenn Mueller PhD

Recovery: In The Recovery Phase, the market is improving and prices and rents begin to increase, although many buyers and developers are still hesitant to proceed. More tenants enter the market and property owners refinance as affordable loan rates become available. Owners tend to improve their properties and work to maximize rental rates. Prices are increasing. This is a very good time to buy because there are still some relative bargains, and demand for space is definitely increasing. New construction is generally limited to build-to-suit, with little to no spec development.

Expansion: During the Expansion Phase, the real estate market is improving and expanding, and equity investors are plentiful. Financing becomes more readily available and the price of real estate may increase more than seen in previous history. Vacancies move towards their lowest point and there is a general sense of well-being, prosperity, and abundance. "Everyone" is talking about buying real estate. This is the best time to sell and the worst time to lease. Rental rates will typically meet the "cost feasible rent rate" for spec development during the Expansion Phase.

Hypersupply: The Hypersupply Phase is when vacancies are increasing and prices begin to fall from the peak of the Expansion Phase. The market has become oversaturated and financing is again becoming less available and more expensive. Investors begin to withdraw from the market as vacancy and delinquency rates rise and prices decline. Foreclosures begin to increase, as some owners are unable to meet financing obligations due to vacancies. These are generally uncertain times and buying, selling, or leasing decisions should be based on specific business needs, unique prime property availability, and individual opportunities.

Recession: The Recession Phase of the market cycle follows a market contraction from the peak of expansion and hyper-supply conditions. During this period, the availability of affordable financing dries up and property prices bottom out. Properties experience higher vacancy rates and owners are challenged to sell, lease, and finance their properties. We also start to see foreclosures increase in the marketplace. Indications that the market is moving out of recession can signal a good time to buy. Many times, property prices fall well below replacement cost, resulting in opportunities for investors with the liquidity and vision to capitalize on bargain prices. This is also one of the best times to lease a property.

Key Takeaways :

- The four distinct phases of the commercial real estate cycle are: Recovery, Expansion, Hypersupply and Recession
- Best case scenario for acquisition, disposition, and leasing is to understand and use market condition awareness in your favor by taking a strategic approach to timing your transactions
- All things being equal, the Recovery Phase is generally the best time to acquire space because there are still some relative bargains, and demand for space is definitely increasing
- All other factors being equal, the Expansion Phase is the best time to sell and the worst time to buy as prices and occupancy begin to peak

Chapter 4:
Show Me the Money
– Capital Markets 101

"Look at market fluctuations as your friend
rather than your enemy; profit from folly
rather than participate in it." – WARREN BUFFETT

Space Market

As we know, the definition of a market is 'a mechanism for the exchange of goods and/or services.' The space market, as it refers to industrial real estate, is the market for the right to use real estate (both land and buildings, and the users of industrial real estate create demand for inventory in the space market.

Changes in supply chains, consumer demand, economic growth, and other business drivers impact the demand for industrial space on a dynamic basis. That demand, when factored against existing inventory or 'supply' of buildings, is what drives changes in occupancy levels and market rents all over the country.

As you can see from the following graphic illustration, that point where the demand curve intersects with the supply curve defines occupancy levels and average market rent for a specific type of industrial space at a given time. As more supply is added, the supply curve shifts to the right, and the point of intersection, or "price equilibrium", moves down the X axis, indicating lower rents. In the event that demand decreases and supply remains constant, we see a similar effect. The demand curve shifts left, and the price equilibrium moves down, driving average rental rates and occupancy down, creating more vacancy in the market. The takeaway is that the relationship between users (demand) and existing inventory (supply) work together to define average market rents and occupancy at any given time.

Space Market

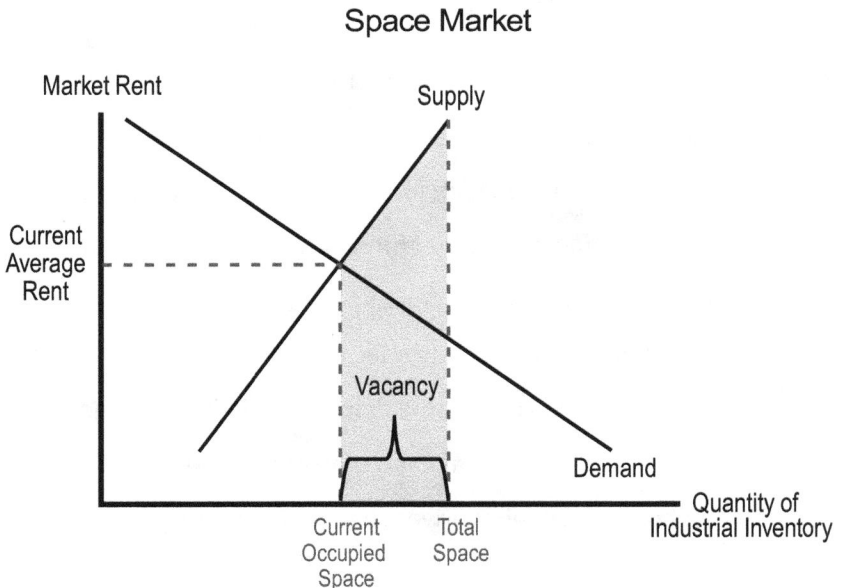

When industrial space becomes scarce enough to drive rents above the cost-feasible rent threshold, developers will create more supply by constructing more industrial space. We normally see this trend occur during the expansion phase and peak out during the hyper-supply phase of the market cycle. Quite typically, lags in new development timing tend to cause supply fluctuations, leading to peaks and then valleys in price and term for the user. That is why it is so important to anticipate, to the best of your ability, your facility needs long-term, so you can make the market cycle work for you and your business and not end up stuck with too much space in a recessionary market.

Capital Markets

At the same time that industrial users drive demand for industrial facilities in the space market, investors are also interested in developing and purchasing buildings that can be leased to businesses for profit. Developers and investors look at the space market and analyze what type of returns they can expect from investment in new buildings. This is largely dependent on projected rents, vacancies, credit risk, and how they believe those factors will change over the holding period of the investment.

So what drives demand for industrial real estate as an investment? Most experts would say that it depends on how the expected return of the investment compares to other investment options with similar risk. If the future outlook for industrial real estate as an asset class looks favorable when compared to other options, investments will flow into industrial assets.

The capital market for investment real estate is mostly defined by the relationship between that supply and demand in any given market. This relationship is what drives the value of the investment space. Most investors value industrial investments in terms of the Net Operating Income (NOI) that they either generated during the last full year or (for new development) the NOI that is expected during the first full year of occupancy. NOI is comprised of all revenue generated by an investment property less its operating expenses in a given period.

The ratio of NOI to the amount investors are willing to pay for the property is referred to as the capitalization rate, or cap rate. The cap rate is a general indicator or guide of what investors are paying, at any given time, for a dollar of NOI. The cap rate can be calculated by dividing the investment's NOI by the current market value.

- Cap Rate = NOI / Value

Alternatively, you can derive value by dividing NOI by a capitalization rate:

- Value = NOI / Cap Rate

Please be aware that a cap rate does not provide you with specifics related to future NOI, risk, or upside opportunity. It does, however, provide a general gauge of what investors are willing to pay for specific property types with specific underlying cash flow streams. For example, Joe and Martha own a modern warehouse leased by a national distributor of consumer goods in a busy industrial park. The corporate tenant has excellent credit ratings and the lease is backed by its corporate guarantee. The current lease term is fifteen years with ten years remaining. NOI for the facility was $280,000 last year. Similar properties in their region have traded at a seven percent cap in the last month. Using the capital market as a guide, Joe and Martha can expect their warehouse to sell for around $4 million. This can be calculated by dividing the last year's NOI ($280,000) by the comparable Cap Rate (7%).

Beyond the simple supply and demand curve for investment warehouse space, many other factors also drive cap rates. Interest rates and availability of capital are important in determining the return the capital market is willing to accept for a given investment. The take-away for the business owner is the understanding of the relationship between the space market and the capital market. Market rents, determined by the space market, establish the NOI that investors realize in the capital market. This determines the price that an investor (in the capital market) is willing to pay for a given income-producing industrial facility, which can be expressed as a cap rate or NOI divided by the value of the investment.

Key Takeaways:

- The demand for industrial real estate as an investment mostly depends on how the expected return on the investment compares to other alternatives with similar risk.

- The delay we see between growth of demand and eventual response in supply is the main driver that causes volatility in real estate market cycles.

- Cap rates provide only a general gauge of what investors are willing to pay per dollar of NOI. The cap rate does not provide specifics related to future NOI, risk, or upside opportunity.

PART 1: ACQUISITION

Chapter 5:
To Lease or Not to Lease?
(Lease vs. Own)

"The indispensable first step to getting the things you want out of life is this: decide what you want." - Ben Stein

So, you've identified that you need industrial space for your business. Your next decision point should be whether to lease or to buy. There are many details to consider when contemplating this decision, beginning with market conditions. In any market or submarket, supply and demand will ebb and flow over time. Timing will always affect your decision to lease versus own based on current or future projected supply of suitable available properties that meet your requirement.

If there are no suitable properties for lease in a given location, then your options are to either buy an existing site or work with a developer willing to construct a build-to-suit and lease the facility to you. The same is true under opposite conditions. For the purposes of comparing lease versus own, this chapter assumes that available properties for lease and for sale are abundant in your market with multiple options to choose from.

There are several advantages and disadvantages for both leasing and owning. Some are strategic, and some are at the tactical level. It is important to understand there is more to the decision-making process than just pure financial analytics. For example, even if financial analysis determines that the ownership option costs less, you might choose to lease because of an exit strategy requirement in your business plan. Whether your business requires you to expand in your existing market, downsize, reconfigure, or move into another geographic region, lease versus buy is an analysis that can significantly change your business' future cash flow, its tax strategy, and net equity on the balance sheet. This chapter explores the advantages and disadvantages that are associated with each option, and different approaches to analyzing the alternatives.

Let's use the example of West Central Food Products (WCFP). WCFP is owned by Jeff, a successful entrepreneur, who developed his company by providing rapid response food processing services primarily to entertainment industry clients in Florida. Jeff had been leasing a facility, continuously expanding to meet the needs of his growing business.

WCFP produced excellent cash flow and had a steady and consistent gross profit margin. As WCFP continued to grow, Jeff began considering his options for a lease renewal coming up in approximately eighteen months. Based on growth in his core business, he knew he was going to need additional space for expansion again. On his way to the office one day, Jeff saw a "for sale" sign on a 50,000 square foot warehouse building my team represented along the main interstate between Tampa and Orlando. That's when Jeff called our office, expressing interest in purchasing the site.

In discussing his situation, it became apparent that Jeff had a very important decision to make. While ownership seemed logical to him, we knew his first step was to work through the lease versus own analysis, exploring both the strategic and financial implications of this important pending change in his business.

Many real estate and finance professionals will tell you that leasing commercial real estate has a lower overall cost than owning. I do not believe that is the case in all situations. The outcome can vary so much from case to case that each situation warrants its own analysis. Before we get into the financial side of the exercise, let's examine some of the advantages and disadvantages of both leasing and property ownership.

Leasing

What is leasing? Leasing is a process where lessors (or landlords) provide lessees (or tenants) the physical use of a real property for a specified period of time without granting a specific ownership interest in the property. Leasing provides certain advantages and disadvantages for you, the business owner.

Leasing Advantages

- Less upfront capital required—Leasing could provide more flexibility for business owners who may need, or prefer, to keep cash invested in the business. In many cases, it makes more sense to invest in the business rather than real estate assets. Less cash required upfront keeps funds available for other uses.

- Operating lease costs are tax-deductible—Lease payments are operating expenses and are fully deductible against earnings. If the lease is a net lease and the lessee pays operating expenses in addition to rent, the operating expenses are deductible as well.

- Excellent financing—Most lease arrangements have fewer restrictions than loan agreements, providing flexible financing. Leasing is often the only available source of financing for a small or marginally profitable firm. Essentially, leasing provides almost 100 percent financing to the tenant with very little upfront cash required for deposit and starts, while most uncollateralized borrowing requires a significant down payment.

- Movement flexibility—Leases are typically much easier to get in and out of than ownership, where the owner must acquire, improve, occupy, and dispose of a site as an alternative to leasing. Lease expiration timeframes and lease options provide both flexibility and benchmarks for the user to plan and reevaluate space needs.

- Focus on core operations—Being a property owner adds a layer of work and responsibility tenants don't have. Leasing allows the business owner to direct more attention to operations without concerns related to facility ownership.

- Cost stabilization—Leasing tends to stabilize and smooth a user's monthly facility expense versus ownership, where annual expenses and major maintenance and repairs can impact the monthly cash flow statement.

Leasing Disadvantages

- Cost—As the industrial market moves into expansion and hyper-supply, market rents go up. If your firm is well capitalized and has a history of strong earnings with good access to capital, it may end up being more expensive to lease than own. Performing a financial analysis is the best way to make that determination.

- No control over your neighbors—Leasing allows no control over other tenants. New neighbor-tenants may not be compatible with your business image, or they may create unexpected demands on your facility. An example would be your landlord leasing the suite next door to a call center, which leads to every parking space in the business park being taken up by its staff.

Leasing Disdvantages (continued)

- No control over your own facility—You may be forced to accept changes to the building that the owner wants, but you oppose. For example, the landlord decides to wait a year to replace the leaky roof, but you want it replaced this quarter because the leak is causing disruption in your operations.

- Limits on what you can do with the facility—You may have problems getting approval for property improvements if the improvements substantially change the leased space or reduce its reuse potential after you are gone. Although the lessee considers the improvements important—such as technological changes necessary to the business, physical changes to accommodate staff, or cosmetic changes to impress customers—the lessor may be reluctant to allow them.

- No equity accumulation or asset appreciation—Leasing does not provide participation in property appreciation.

Owning

Owning is a way for you to obtain full physical and economic use of a property in perpetuity. If you own a commercial property in the United States, you are generally free to use the property as you wish, within the limits of the law. Owning has some clear advantages, and also disadvantages. Here are some to consider when analyzing whether to lease or buy.

Ownership Advantages

- Control—As the owner, you have the right to operate your facility however you wish (again, within the limits of applicable laws). You can invest as much or as little as you wish, and carry out strategies that suit your specific interests and support your business plan objectives.
- Stable investment—Overall, real estate can be a great place to invest your money in the long term. As Mark Twain pointed out, "Buy land, they aren't making it anymore." Owning commercial real estate can be an excellent hedge against inflation and a good way to diversify your investment portfolio.
- Accumulation of equity—As the owner of commercial real estate, you are entitled to all the appreciation in its value.
- Potential tax benefits—You gain tax savings from cost-recovery deductions and the mortgage interest expense during the entire holding period.
- Potential Income—You can rent out a portion of the property to other users, if you wish, thereby providing an additional source of income to you and your business.

- Pride of ownership—You reap the intangible benefit that results from pride and status perceived as a result of your business owning its own facility.

Ownership Disadvantages

- Distraction from core business—Being the facility/property owner can divert energy and take time away from managing your core business.

- Capital required upfront—The initial investment of the down payment and other improvement costs tie up cash that could otherwise be used to fund company operations and primary business requirements.

- Interest rate risk—Depending on financing terms, ownership could be subject to increased costs of capital associated with an increase in interest rates. Your company's ability to obtain financing at favorable rates is not just a function of creditworthiness, but also the availability of financing in the capital markets.

- Asset Value Fluctuation—While in the long run, commercial property valuations have risen, there is always a chance that the value of your facility may go down. If you are forced to sell during a recessionary period, you could end up having to sell below the basis of your investment.

- Risk exposure—Ownership can be subjected to facility related risks of environmental issues, structural issues, and other building-related matters. All of these concerns can be investigated and mitigated upfront by doing due diligence. Other concerns that cannot be resolved prior to acquisition could be exposure to potential damage during ownership, building obsolescence, and the lack of liquidity associated with commercial real estate ownership as compared to other forms of financial investment.

- Balance sheet debt—The financial liability of a mortgage can negatively impact your balance sheet, by increasing long-term liabilities and negatively affecting your debt-to-equity ratio. This can have a further negative impact on obtaining other forms of financing at favorable rates and terms for your business.

- Lack of flexibility—It is possible the facility could be inflexible, and difficult or impossible to expand or downsize, based on requirements of the business. In this situation with a lease, you could simply move on to the next facility at end of term or seek early termination or modification options. When you own a facility that doesn't work for your business, your options are more limited.

When deciding whether to buy or lease an industrial property, it's important to understand all potential risks and, of course, the upside of both options. The last thing you want to do is buy a property and then realize a year or two later that you would have been better off leasing—or

LEASE

Advantages

- Less Upfront Capital Required to Occupy
- Operating Lease Expenses Are Tax-Deductible
- Excellent Source of Financing
- Movement Flexibility for the Business
- Facility Expense Cost Stabilization

Disadvantages

- Exposure to Rate Escalations
- No Control Over Your Neighbors
- No Control Over Landlord Actions That Affect Your Business
- Limits on What You Can Do With the Facility
- No Equity Accumulation or Asset Appreciation

OWN

Advantages

- 👍 Total Control
- 👍 Stable Investment
- 👍 Accumulation of Equity
- 👍 Tax Benefits from Depreciation
- 👍 Potential Income
- 👍 Pride of Ownership

Disadvantages

- 👎 Distraction from Core Business
- 👎 Capital Required Upfront
- 👎 Interest Rate Risk
- 👎 Asset Value Fluctuation
- 👎 Physical Plant Risk Exposure
- 👎 Possible Negative Impact to Balance Sheet
- 👎 Lack Of Flexibility

vice versa. By exploring some of the advantages and disadvantages to both options, hopefully, you have a good idea of how your specific situation is impacted by the pros and cons of each scenario.

Qualitative Analysis

Now that we understand the advantages and disadvantages of leasing and owning, let's take some time to discover some tools that can aid in the actual decision making process.

In the WCFP example, the very first action we took was to conduct a face-to-face, thorough consultative interview with Jeff. We utilized our team 'industrial space requirements protocol' to guide the discussion. Our protocol includes process-driven tools that allow us, as consultants, to understand exactly what type of facility the customer needs, and the requirements of that facility.

We go beyond the actual physical characteristics and requirements of the building itself and incorporate an understanding of the strategic direction of the business. It allows us, as real estate advisors, to "think like an owner" and really become business advisors.

Some of the topics discussed with Jeff during the meeting included:
- His growth plans for the next five to ten years, specifically those that will affect his space requirements.

- His future business vision, beyond this other contract that he's landed.

- His strategic plans for the company.

- His geographic needs in terms of where the facilities are located, the size of the facility, and the business lines he'll be servicing. We also consider changing technologies that will affect space requirements— such as new racking systems, manufacturing techniques, safety requirements, or computer software like warehouse management systems that could change the optimal business configuration.

- His exit strategy, both in terms of when he plans to exit the business and how his plan relates to ownership or leasing of the facility.

- His strategic position on internal investment in facilities. Paying for any expansion or change internally, through organic operations or using outside sources of finance, impacts the overall long-term direction of the business.

Understanding the answers to these questions was vital to understanding the capital structure of Jeff's business. Anticipating the need for growth capital, we discussed whether Jeff wanted to employ organic capital toward this expansion or if he wanted to consider, explore, and understand all potential financing options. Armed with detailed information related to the clients' strategic direction, we can confidently move into the qualitative analysis portion of the decision making process.

The qualitative analysis allows you to assemble and rate all of your subjective decision factors on one list. When facing a tough decision, I recommend making a list of your criteria for each alternative and customizing it with your priorities. All of your criteria should be listed, assigned a weight, and then scored on a scale of 1 to 10. Multiply the weight by the score for each criteria item and then sum the total at the bottom of the sheet for each alternative. The greater sum should provide you with some insight and at least give you a feel for which way to lean in your decision making exercise.

For example, in Jeff's analysis of his needs for WCFP, flexibility in configuration of his facility was extremely important because his packaging requirements and line configuration had to remain flexible to meet the changing needs of his clients. So, we assigned a high weight ranking to flexibility, which translated to higher scores for the ownership option. This fact, combined with the weight of his other criteria, made it clear for Jeff that from a qualitative perspective, ownership was the right option for his situation. It is important to seek input from others that can provide insight. Work with your advisor or project team to define what really matters to you, weight all of your decision criteria, then score the options by internally addressing differences and concerns as a part of the decision making process.

Financial Analysis

We've completed your qualitative analysis and have narrowed your list of suitable properties to one or two primary options. Now it's time to take a look at the financial analysis. Since a lease provides a form of financing for your company, it should be analyzed as a financing alternative compared to purchasing with cash or some combination of purchase financing.

Since both options generate a series of cash flows over a specified period of time, I recommend utilizing the net present value (NPV) method for comparative financial analysis. The NPV method is the simplest approach and distills each option down to its periodic cash flow after taxes. You will need to know or determine your company's after-tax discount rate, in order to calculate an NPV for each alternative.

Most large corporate industrial users will utilize their after-tax weighted average cost of capital as their discount rate, while most small to medium business owners and private investors prefer to plug in their "opportunity" cost (after tax) or what they can make as a return on an annual basis (after tax) in competing alternative investments. Once the current NPV for each option is calculated, compare the values, and if you need assistance with this analysis, please make sure to contact a qualified commercial real estate advisor with experience and training in financial analysis. For the purposes of this analysis, the greater value is always the better economic choice.

Some of the key assumptions, in addition to the discount rate, that are required when modeling your financial analysis are:

- Holding period—How long do you intend to occupy or hold on to the property? What is the anticipated need for your business, and how does this facility fit into your business plan? Whether you intend to hold the facility long term (ten to twenty years) or sell it or lease it out after five years, it is important to analyze comparable timeframes when considering lease versus own.

- Lease/financing terms—What are the key assumptions for financing? What is the required Loan to Value (LTV) percent? What are the interest rate, amortization, and term of the loan? Lease escalators, pass-throughs, and other tenant expenses must be factored into the comparison.

- Taxes—Calculations should include income tax, real estate tax, use tax, and other types of taxes. Also, there may be tax incentives such as depreciation expense, rental expense, interest expense, and others that must be factored into the analysis. The tax implications will vary for each situation, but must be considered and included in the financial analysis. Since there are various tax impacts between leasing versus owning, it is important to analyze financial implications on an after-tax basis.

The decision to lease versus own ultimately comes down to two things: strategic implications and economics. In the case of Jeff with WCFP, we decided that the best course of action was to own. The NPV analysis showed that owning over the ten-year period for his projected use of the facility yielded a net present value of $750,000 more than his leasing alternative. Additionally, from qualitative perspective, owning the facility allowed WCFP the flexibility and control needed to configure and reconfigure its line in a way that wouldn't have been possible in a leased facility.

For the sake of good business decision-making, I always recommend that my clients put together an advisory team to assist in developing lease versus own analysis. With good qualitative and quantitative analysis, you can make an informed decision based on the best information available at that point in time.

Key Takeaways:

- Lease versus buy is an analysis that can significantly change your business's future cash flow, its tax strategy, and net equity on the balance sheet.

- Advantages to leasing: Could provide more flexibility, operating lease costs are tax-deductible, most lease arrangements have fewer restrictions than loan agreements, and flexible financing.

- Disadvantages to leasing: Rental rate escalation risk. You may be forced to accept changes to the building that the owner wants, but you oppose.

- Advantages to owning: Owning is a way for you to obtain full physical and economic use of a property in perpetuity, and real estate can be a great place to invest your money in the long term.

- Disadvantages to owning: Additional obligations distract you from running your business, and capital is required.

- It's important to consider market conditions for sale and lease options, define specific space acquisition strategy, and perform qualitative, financial, and market analysis before deciding on a course of action.

Chapter 6:
Leasing – Know Your Options!

"Risk comes from not knowing

what you're doing." - Warren Buffet

Leasing decisions not only can have a significant impact on operating budgets, but can also have major strategic impact on a firm's success. This is not a decision to make lightly, and I always recommend examining all options very carefully. The first question we should explore is, should you stay in your current location or relocate? Initially, relocating may seem like a huge endeavor, but the effort could be well worth the investment.

In some cases, we find that staying in the current location is not the best option in the long run. I encourage business owners to seriously consider their strategic direction and goals, and then decide if their existing location supports where they are headed in three, five, even ten years. Working through the what-if's with a trusted commercial real estate advisor can help you think through the possibilities.

Should I Stay?

If your existing facility satisfies your current and long-term business needs, but you are nearing the end of your lease term, you may consider renewing the lease. If so, it is important to bring a trusted commercial real estate broker and advisor to represent you in negotiating the lease renewal. This is an area where I see many business owners sacrifice opportunities to significantly improve their lease terms and rates because they are not aware of everything up for negotiation.

Most business owners I know are really good at what they do. So good, in fact, that they believe they don't need assistance with lease negotiations—they believe they can handle it themselves. What they don't realize is how much a good commercial real estate advisor can improve the outcome. Negotiating through a real estate broker keeps the tenant at arm's length and provides greater leverage in negotiations. A good advisor's market-specific intelligence will aid in negotiating the best terms and most concessions in the leasing deal.

Business owners are usually great negotiators in their own businesses, but they aren't always familiar with the impact of commercial real estate leases. They don't fully understand terms such as termination options, right-of-first-refusal for expansion space, moving allowances, and caps on operating expenses. These are concepts that can have a significant impact on your business. A good broker/advisor takes the time to understand your business needs and goals, and how they relate to the lease or acquisition. As a result, he or she is able to help you negotiate the best terms and conditions for your situation.

You may think you're facing just a "simple" lease renewal, but even then there are as many available concessions and negotiation points as in the initial lease. Renewing tenants are far more profitable to landlords than new ones. A good broker/advisor has a thorough understanding of current market concessions, comparable rates, and other market indicators. All these help leverage your renewal options if you decide to stay in your current facility.

It is also important to understand comparable rates and terms when negotiating a renewal. Business owners may be able to find rates, prices, and availabilities of some transactions on the Internet, but what about "off market" availabilities, typical lease concessions, properties soon to be available, or other myriad lease covenants? Also, I've discovered that most of my clients don't have the tools to prepare a detailed financial analysis of costs associated with each potential option—rent, operating expenses, improvement allowances, moving allowances, etc. For example, if considering a lease renewal option, you should include expansion and contraction costs, as well as the cost of any reconfiguration of your existing workspace.

In 99 percent of the cases I have seen, business owners negotiating their own lease renewals without representation end up wasting valuable time from their core business, and they spend a significant amount of effort negotiating without the tools and knowledge of a well-qualified commercial real estate representative. It just doesn't make sense, when all of these services are available to the business, at no additional cost. One solution is to consider utilizing the services of a tenant representation (tenant rep) broker.

> There is a common misconception that hiring a tenant rep broker costs the tenant extra.

There is a common misconception that hiring a tenant rep broker costs the tenant extra. In reality, the current industry standard is for the landlord to pay all brokerage fees for new lease acquisitions and renewals. In a majority of all cases, representation will not impact the cost of your lease.

Even if you have a great relationship with your landlord, your interests run contrary to one another. A broker representative is positioned to push harder for a better deal than you, as tenant, can achieve because it is an arm's length transaction. The broker is an effective buffer in preserving that good relationship you have with the landlord. Remember, *you* are more important to your landlord than he or she is to you!

I interviewed Dwight Hotchkiss, President of Colliers' Brokerage Services in the United States, to draw from his over twenty-five years of experience on this subject. Dwight is responsible for the Colliers National Brokerage Services platform, encompassing 23 practice groups with more than 600 brokers across the country. He has worked with hundreds of clients over his career with differing situations and had some very valuable advice to offer. An expert in national industrial trends, I asked him to share some of the main reasons why an industrial user with a facility leasing need should engage a commercial real estate advisor early in the process.

Dwight: *I like to think a good broker is going to be a great advisor to the client. That means they understand that client's business and help to drive real estate decisions based on their business needs and the growth of the business. The cost of real estate is only a small portion of what goes on in a real estate transaction.*

A client who engages a professional advisor early on will get the benefit of advice on location incentives, propriety and insightful market intel, and a good understanding of the motivations of landlords in the marketplace. It may be that they have a history and are aware of why one landlord may give them a better deal than another. It's based on an understanding of what goes on in a marketplace in the sense of comparable transactions or recent transactions. Their intellectual capital and resources will save a user a tremendous amount of time and a tremendous amount of money that can be directed toward business growth.

Q: With changes in the flow of information through the Internet in the past decade, we see more owners and users going to the Internet for information and attempting to handle their real estate transactions in-house. When you see that type of scenario, what advice can you give a business owner or industrial user contemplating whether to work with a broker or do the transaction on his own?

Dwight: *Well, you can also go into the web and find medical information, but are you really going to make a medical decision about something based on what you read on the web? Or are you going to see a doctor with the expertise to advise you in the right way for your health?*

Similarly, sure, you can look on the web and find available properties and land information, but is that really comparable to having someone knowledgeable to represent you and negotiate or deal with contracts?

Q: Over the years, you've seen decisions made, despite the talent available to represent businesses and business owners, when managers did attempt to handle these transactions in house. Can you remember or recall any such situation where the result turned out poorly for the user? Where they attempted to do it on their own and it just didn't work out?

Dwight: *Once, when I was an industrial brokerage professional, I had a situation with a regional import-export company that focused on the West Coast and had grown large enough to compete in numerous markets in that region. With one particular facility, they had a lease coming to an end within six months, requiring a decision as to whether or not to renew. Based on how long they had been around in the market, they thought they knew what was available in the geographic area and didn't need to hire a broker. Instead they negotiated a lease directly with a landlord and signed a ten year lease – which very few people did at the time – for, I believe, 300,000 square foot building, and they signed at an above-market rent. Additionally, they didn't have the sprinkler calculation required for their product type to stack to the height they needed in the building, and they also had no tenant improvement dollars given to them.*

Over the term of the lease, they probably overpaid by a half a million dollars; it cost them that much. Again, having an advisor representing you that has the knowledge to bring in an third party expert to help with things like sprinkler calculations or building inspections will save you headaches and money that you can invest into your business in the future.

Q: That's a really good example and a cautionary tale for those thinking about going it alone. What do you think motivated that business, Dwight? What do you think caused them to kind of go out on their own, to try to handle it in-house?

Dwight: *I believe they were thinking that, by not paying a brokers commission, the money could go back into the transaction and lower the rent and make them a great deal. In reality, however, broker's commissions are such a small percentage of the overall cost of a deal.*

Clearly, working with a trusted real estate advisor in any real estate transaction is valuable and can save your business more than just money. A good advisor will help protect your business from unnecessary risk and help you sleep better at night.

Or Should I Go?

An upcoming lease expiration can offer you an opportunity to transform your business through relocation. After conducting your needs assessment, you may consider relocating if growth and market conditions support that option. If your current facility is too small, too large, obsolete, or non-functional, a new facility can provide a great opportunity to increase productivity, eliminate waste, tap new labor pools, reduce logistics costs, and increase employee morale. Additionally, market conditions or municipal business development incentives may support the case for relocation.[i]

Whether you decide to stay or go, knowledge is key. Take the time to examine and understand the situation in your current facility. Review all your options, and assess the current market conditions to understand the overall opportunity for relocation. The period of time required to select a property, conduct the lease negotiations, and relocate takes a minimum of six months. Depending on the size of your business and the current amount of supply in the marketplace, I recommend beginning the process a year in advance of the lease expiration. For a large business, it can take twenty-four months or more to complete the relocation process.

When considering whether it makes sense to potentially stay in your existing facility versus relocating, think about the 'blend and extend' option. I recently met with industry expert Jack Rosenberg at an industrial conference in Newport Beach, CA where Jack took time to discuss some of the specifics of this strategy. A Principal at Colliers International and the National Director of the Colliers Logistics and Transportation Solutions Group, Jack is one of the top industrial producers in the nation and specializes in site acquisition, leasing, sales and build-to-suits for industrial users and developers. Jack works for some of the most prestigious clients in the industry. To say that he knows a thing or two about leasing strategy is putting it mildly. For the benefit of our readers, I asked him about blend and extend as a strategy for the industrial user. Here are some highlights of our conversation:

Q: Can you provide the reader with a good definition of what 'blend and extend' is and how it can benefit the user?

Jack: *Under a blend and extend strategy, you go to the landlord before the lease is up to trade a lease extension for concessions. In the best scenario, the concessions start during the existing lease term. You have to really understand where the market is, as well as competing alternatives, and the landlord's specific situation and appetite for an extension. Blend and extend is much more difficult to achieve with a meaningful effect in a tight market with historically low vacancies of industrial properties across the US. Blend and extend works best where the market is in equilibrium or there's a slight oversupply of space. It doesn't have to be much.*

For example, we just completed a transaction in the Chicago metro area for a blend and extend on a very specialized facility. It's a 115,000 square foot tin plate steel service center with some very specialized features like a 13" thick floor to hold heavy loads and 35-foot deep slack take-up pits for slitting the rolls of tin plate. My client had two years before the end of their 15-year lease. We approached the landlord and said, "We'll extend the lease by ten years, but we want to start the discount now."

In this scenario, we didn't only focus on rent. In the original 15-year lease that my client signed, they assumed responsibility for the roof. So during the 'blend and extend' negotiations, we explained to the landlord that we were two years in advance of the lease ending, and we were working on potential options to move. The tenant, our client, could have a new building built and, based on broad economics, the rent would be competitive or perhaps cheaper, but they wouldn't have roof replacement responsibilities.

The strategy worked, and we were able to not only get the rent down – with a little bit of free rent extending the term out - but we also convinced the landlord to take the roof responsibilities and do some other maintenance items. So with blend and extend, the tenant benefits, and the landlord benefits as well by locking in an additional ten-year term with a strong credit tenant. It's a win-win for both, and the party I represent (the tenant) simply signs a piece of paper, the lease amendment. There is no downtime, no moving distribution, no additional operational costs, and no capital costs to move, meaning they save money day one.

Q: And they're not on the hook for the roof.

Jack: *Yes. [In the process] We look at a lease abstract, and we look at all the maintenance items in the building, and we basically say to the landlord, "You have to assume that they're going to leave and that you're going to have to do this stuff anyway. Why should you treat my tenant, who has the ability to leave and not have any of that responsibility, differently than you would a new tenant?"*

Q: In an expanding market, if there are certain assets that were going to recycle (be sold) by an institutional owner, that could be a big incentive for that owner to do a blend and extend if they knew they wanted to keep their occupancy at a certain level in order to successfully recycle the asset, right?

Jack: *Right. In another example, we once represented a tenant in a million square foot building in Nashville. At the time, all the publicly traded real estate companies were just trying to survive. The landlord went public before the recession, bought whatever they could in order to appear meaningful in a public market, then, through the recession, started to say, "What kind of company do we want to be?"*

This particular landlord changed from just wanting to bulk up to go public to focusing on major distribution markets - and not just be everything to everybody everywhere. We knew that holding a building in Nashville was not going to be meaningful to them and they were going to want to get out of it. We knew that selling that building was going to be an important part of their equation. We also learned that this building was the biggest building the landlord owned, and that the rent was meaningful enough to be reported as 3 percent of their total rent receipts. That helped us get a better deal for our tenant. In fact, they had the ability to buy or lease, and they ended up buying that building.

Doing that kind of deep dive on behalf of your tenants, really focusing on the transaction, is critical. In this case, we were able to find a great deal of intel on the landlord prior to negotiating because the company was public. That information helped us get a better result. In that case, we beat the tenant's internal projections by 15 percent on the project.

Leading the Team

The internal team should be led by you, as the owner, or by a key senior employee. This team should be supported by other decision makers and influencers, including department leaders and key staff. Additionally, I recommend including a professional real estate advisor early on. He or she will become a critical part of the project team, providing you access to proprietary market data, potential alternatives, and the financial implications of various scenarios. Of course, you may encounter scenarios where you are tempted to manage the lease acquisition process without the support of a commercial real estate advisor. Regardless of how you choose to proceed, you can mitigate some risk by being aware of some of the most common pitfalls we see in the leasing process:

Top Seven Mistakes Made by Tenants in the Leasing Process

1. Beginning the leasing process too late, which puts the tenant at a negotiating disadvantage.
2. Not designating a project manager as the internal single point of contact.
3. Focusing mainly on the direct financial costs without considering the qualitative or strategic costs.
4. Lacking intel regarding off-market upcoming availabilities. Most of the time, the best deals are secured well in advance of space vacancies.
5. Not leveraging current market knowledge to negotiate the most favorable terms and tenant improvement allowance.
6. Not building flexibility into facility plan for future expansion or contraction.
7. Not pulling the trigger quickly once a decision is made, and consequently missing opportunities.

Types of Leases

There are several types of leases commonly utilized in commercial real estate. It is important to understand these different leases in order to properly compare and contrast them when analyzing and negotiating for your company. There are full-service gross leases, modified gross leases, and net leases. Most industrial facility leases are either modified gross or net. These forms of leases refer to roles and responsibilities, and how various costs are paid for between the landlord and the tenant.

First, let's take a look at full-service gross leases. Under this arrangement, the tenant makes one monthly payment to the landlord, and the landlord is responsible for maintenance, taxes, insurance, and utilities. In most cases, the tenant is responsible for his share of any increase in operating expenses over the term of the lease.

Modified gross leases (or industrial gross leases) are commonly utilized in industrial facilities. They are comparable to full-service gross leases, but some specific operating expenses are paid directly by the tenant. Normally, tenants pay their own utilities and janitorial services. However, every situation is a little different, and many times these costs and responsibilities are negotiable.

Similar to gross leases, net leases appear in many varieties. Net leases require the tenant to pay some or all expenses directly related to the property. These expenses can include property taxes, insurance, maintenance, repairs, utilities, janitorial services, and other operating costs. The three most common net leases are:

- **Single Net (SN)**—The tenant pays a lump sum base rent plus property taxes. The landlord is responsible for all other operating expenses.

- **Double Net (NN)**—The tenant pays a lump sum base rent plus property taxes and insurance. The landlord is responsible for all other operating expenses.

- **Triple Net (NNN)**—Triple net leases are most commonly used for single tenant industrial facilities. The tenant is almost completely responsible for every operating cost related to the building. In addition to paying for taxes, maintenance, and insurance, tenants are also responsible for all costs associated with occupancy, including utilities, personal property taxes, and janitorial services. In most cases, the landlord is responsible for the roof and the structure.

Other Lease Considerations

Regardless of the type of lease you are considering for industrial space, it's important to clarify specifically what you will and will not be responsible for. Remember, in many situations, cost responsibilities and pass-throughs are negotiable. Also, in multi-tenant buildings, it is important to clarify parking allocations upfront, to avoid issues and disputes down the road.

It's also important to remember that, the longer the term, the more valuable the lease is to the landlord. Generally, the building owner will offer more tenant improvement allowance, rent abatement, and other concessions in exchange for longer term leases backed by excellent credit. This provides a higher certainty of positive cash flow from the owner's investment and, generally, landlords are willing to make concessions up front to guarantee that positive cash flow.

Tenants, on the other hand, prefer flexibility. They want the ability to remain nimble as the businesses scale up and down in order to meet demand and other business requirements. To capitalize on the landlord's appetite for length of term while still maintaining some flexibility, some of our clients assume long-term leases with cancellation options. Typically, landlords will require some form of compensation if the option is exercised, such as an early cancellation fee, to minimize loss from vacancy and to cover initial startup costs.

Some of our clients have rapidly changing business models and simply cannot commit to a specific space for more than three to five years. They pay more for rent and generally receive fewer concessions, but they have more mobility and flexibility associated with the shorter term.

Landlords typically prefer long-term leases and will offer more attractive base rent rates and more concessions in exchange for lease terms of ten years or greater. Most businesses, however, prefer flexibility, especially given the rapidly changing economic environment we are operating in. If you fall in this category, I would advise pursuing a hybrid scenario, such as a longer term lease with cancellation options, if the landlord is willing to consider.

You also can request an option or options to extend the lease at a rental rate structure, which you should take great care to negotiate up front. While an option is your right, not an obligation to accept or decline in the future, it does create an obligation to the landlord. What you should focus on is negotiating an option to continue per existing lease terms, or to continue at a rate adjusted by a certain percentage. Beware of options to continue under prevailing market conditions at the time of option renewal, as these options can put you at a disadvantage, especially if the definition of 'prevailing market rate' is not negotiated in your favor.

Another consideration is what happens if you need to stay longer than the lease term. A holdover provision can cover this scenario. A holdover typically involves staying in the space for an extra month or two beyond the lease expiration date. Most of the time, landlords set holdover rental rates at between 150 and 200 percent of the last month's rent, but this is a negotiable item that you or your advisor can discuss when negotiating lease terms.

Standard Lease Terms

Lease documents are typically lengthy and can require specialized experience to understand. After reading through one—if you can stay awake—you will probably have questions about what some of the terms actually mean and about the implications for your business. A simple, overlooked issue or misunderstood clause could become a major expense down the road. That is why I always recommend hiring legal counsel specifically experienced in commercial real estate lease review and negotiations.

We regularly encounter situations where tenants relied on legal advice from general counsel or some other type of legal specialist and live to regret that decision. I repeat: retain legal counsel that is experienced specifically in commercial real estate lease review and negotiations.

> Retain legal counsel that is experienced specifically in commercial real estate lease review and negotiations.

Here is a list of lease terms you are likely to see in standard leases:[ii]

- **Abatement**—Often and commonly referred to as free rent or early occupancy and may occur outside, or in addition to, the primary term of the lease.
- **Building Consent**—Approval from the relevant authorities for carrying out building work on the premises, usually for tenant improvements.

- **Cap and Collar**—A term and method used in some market review clauses. It is a mechanism that puts a "cap" or maximum amount on how much the rent can be increased, while the "collar" is the maximum the rent can decrease on the rental rate review date. As industrial leasing markets strengthen, these review methods are more difficult to negotiate.

- **Expense Stop**—An agreed dollar amount of taxes and operating expense (expressed for the building as a whole or on a square foot basis) over which the tenant will pay its prorated share of increases. This limits the landlord's risk by establishing a ceiling on certain expenses that landlord is responsible for.

- **Estoppel Certificate**—A signed statement certifying that certain statements of fact are correct as of the date of the statement and can be relied upon by a third party, including a prospective lender or purchaser. In the context of a lease, a statement by a tenant identifying that the lease is in effect and certifying that no rent has been prepaid and that there are no known outstanding defaults by the landlord.

- **Default**—Defined specifically in each individual lease agreement and generally occurs when the tenant fails to pay the proper rent or fulfill other obligations under the lease within a specified period of time.

- **Lessee**— Also known as the tenant, the legal entity, company, or person whose name appears on the formal lease document as the occupier or user of space, and which binds the lessee to the terms and conditions stated therein.

- **Lessor**—The party whose name appears as landlord or owner of the property on the formal lease document.
- **Make Good**—The lessee's obligation to return the premises to original conditions prior to expiration of the lease.
- **Net Rent, Gross Rent**—Net rent is only the actual cost of leasing the property. Gross rent is the rental rate that includes the lessee's share of the operating expenses (e.g., property taxes, insurance, property management). Lease terms such as modified or industrial gross, Net-Net, Triple Net, etc. describe different proportions of operating expenses that will be paid by the tenant.
- **Operating Expenses**—All secondary expenses other than rent. These include insurance, property taxes, operation, and upkeep and/or maintenance of the building, including air conditioning, maintenance, common area cleaning, security, and electricity.
- **Quiet Enjoyment**—A right to the undisturbed use and enjoyment of real property by a tenant.
- **Rent Review**—The method by which rent can vary during the term of the lease. This can be a market rate review, a predetermined figure (such as three percent) or a rate fixed to an index such as the CPI. The review structure is agreed upon prior to lease commencement.

- **Resource Consent**—Approval from the local governing author-ity with regard to zoning or changes in the permitted use of the premises.
- **Right of Renewal**—The lessee's right to renew a lease, prior to expiration of the initial lease, for an agreed upon period of time.
- **Statutory Expenses**—Statutory expenses include costs such as municipal rates, water and sewer rates, and usage charges.
- **Sublease/Assignment**—The mechanism under the lease provi-sions that allow the lessee to find a suitable replacement tenant. This is subject to the lessor's approval and, unless specifically stated, does not limit the lessee's legal responsibilities during the lease term.

Lease Process

Determine Future Space Needs[iii]

You should integrate your company's long-range business plan into your decision making process for leases spanning five years or greater. I find it helpful to bring together the company's key staff and advisors and work through the development of a requirement summary. The process begins with an open brainstorming exercise facilitated by the appointed project leader. I recommend using some or all of the follow-ing questions as a guide to facilitating the discussion. Once you work through the strategic discussion, the project leader will be prepared to develop your company's requirement summary and decision matrix. Examples of these tools are available at www.warehouseveteran.com.

Strategic Questions to Consider for Space Planning

- **Core values**—What are your brand values and how do they affect your facility requirements?

- **Logistics**—How will your location impact your logistics and transportation costs?

- **Industry change**—What disruptive changes are happening, or might happen, in your industry that could affect facility requirements during the term of the lease?

- **Future growth plans**—What is your businesses growth trajectory? Are you considering acquiring or merging with other firms?

- **Technology**—What new technology is or will become available during the term of your lease?

- **Stakeholders**—What effect will moving have on your customers, vendors, and staff?

- **Labor pool**—What are the long-term prospects for the quality and availability of employees?

The point of this exercise is to begin identifying key strategic considerations prior to the decision making phase. If you are factoring in the details of workplace considerations only during the design and construction phase of your tenant improvement buildout, only minor gains in productivity and efficiency of your facility will be possible. By working through the process in advance, you achieve the maximum benefit by building key facility components that support your business plan in the space planning process.

Now that you have considered the strategic implications of your business plan, it is time to develop your requirement summary. At this stage, it is important to involve key internal decision makers. Put together a team with a breadth of skills and give them the resources to drive the project. Involve your human resources and finance experts, who will be aware of specific trends that may influence your requirements and decisions. Their involvement from the outset will help clarify and focus your brief and also achieve internal buy-in. Collaborate with your plant and facility managers, manufacturing engineers, and operations manager. This will ensure that you base your plan on the best information available.

If your plan is to relocate, you should include vendors who supply and maintain your major machinery, so you can factor in expenses related to upgrading power, transporting and recalibrating equipment, and servicing equipment onsite.

Step 1—Document Your Requirements

A well-prepared lease requirement summary clearly defines needs and distills them into the property requirements. The requirement summary will save you time and effort by allowing your team to focus only on properties that meet the defined criteria.

The requirement summary also creates a mechanism for you to evaluate and compare options. Begin by defining what is and is not working in your existing facility. Include those components you believe are important in your summary. Some of the standard criteria we normally include in our requirement summaries are:

- Size of facility
- Percentage of office, warehouse, manufacturing space
- Utility requirements (natural gas, power, water, and data requirements)
- Size of workforce (maximum and minimum)
- Style and appearance
- Truck court layout and radius
- Parking requirement
- Ceiling clear height
- Loading doors (type and number)
- Climate control
- Access to transportation networks
- Operating hours
- Security and access
- Lease structure preferences
- Company specific requirements
- Budget
- Local and state incentives

I recommend constructing a decision matrix that ranks each factor in terms of importance, as you may have to compromise on some items, depending on the options available. You can also assign a point value to each factor, with more points attributed to the factors having greater importance. The decision matrix template at www.warehouseveteran.com provides a good start for the process. Your commercial real estate advisor also will be a good resource, to guide you through the evaluation process. He or she should provide expertise and experience in the evaluation and decision making process, factoring in the specifics of local market knowledge.

During this phase, it is important to research and understand local market conditions and pricing. By knowing the market and submarket vacancy rates, property values, inventory projections, current rental rates, and tenant incentives, you are in a better position to evaluate proposals and, ultimately, negotiate the very best lease for your company. Your commercial real estate advisor can provide you with a market presentation describing these factors in both your local market and in specific submarkets that you identify as most desirable.

Step 2—Identify and Evaluate Market Alternatives

At this point, you should release your summary to the market and begin to identify available options. There are several commercial real estate marketing databases that are a source of properties available for lease. Currently, the main commercial real estate databases are CoStar, Loopnet, and Xceligent.

To avoid dealing with multiple agents and owners, request that your real estate professional advisor approach the market on your behalf. Through proprietary market knowledge and a well-established network of agents and owners, your advisor should act as a single point of contact to uncover all suitable space opportunities. Your advisor is also in the best position to assist in discussions with your existing landlord regarding lease renewal options. He or she can keep you at arm's length and also provide an advantage during negotiations by bringing suitable alternatives into the equation, thereby reducing the landlord's leverage.

Step 3—Evaluate and Prepare a Short List

Once you have identified all available facilities that meet your criteria from the requirement summary, focus on narrowing the list by considering timing, financial, and other incentives that may be offered. Assigning weights to each category using the site selection decision matrix is helpful at this time to sort out your alternatives. An example of this tool is included in the appendix and can be downloaded at www.warehouseveteran.com.

The goal of the site selection decision matrix is to narrow down to a short list of three to five properties. If you are still considering a renewal in your existing space, this option should be included right along with the others for side-by-side comparison.

Again, assign a weight to each of the decision criteria you include in your requirement summary. Evaluate the options against the summary, assigning a score for each measurable item. The goal is to ensure that you are matching each property's benefits to your stated business objectives. Once you have scored each property in each category, multiply the score times the weight and summarize the score for each alternative at the bottom of the sheet. Consider eliminating your lowest scoring properties from consideration at this point.

Step 4—Visit and Inspect Your Short List

At this stage, it is very important to physically visit each site. Get a true feel for the location, the facility's layout, and the functionality of the site. If you are working with a commercial real estate advisor, he or she will arrange site tours and coordinate entry into all facilities on the list. If possible, bring along your key decision makers and other critical advisors who can be helpful at this stage, including your architect/engineer, space planner, contractor, and plant engineer. Be sure to record key observations about the facility as they relate to your requirement summary.

It is also important to conduct design site audits of the short-listed options so you can begin to determine potential workspace efficiency gains for each property. This process can also generate sample tenant improvement (TI) designs prior to any agreement on terms, enabling you to compare your options based on both financial and nonfinancial criteria. Here are some of the items your architect should include during this critical evaluation phase:

- Manage the pre-design process, including a review of local authority approvals and code requirements.
- Prepare preliminary concept designs.
- Assess items suitable for re-use in the improved plant or facility.
- Provide an opinion of likely tenant improvement costs.

Step 5—Financial Analysis

Once you have determined your short list and toured those facilities, you most likely have narrowed the choices down to two or three. The next step is to request a proposal from each owner (RFP), to compare the financial considerations of each. Standard financial measures of leases for comparison include:

- Gross effective rent per square foot.
- Gross and net rent per square foot.
- Total occupancy cost per employee.

When evaluating lease terms, you must take into account all incentives, pass-throughs, and escalators over the life of the lease to accurately calculate the gross effective rent per square foot. Some examples include free rent, allowances for tenant improvements, rent hikes, and pass-through provisions.

It is important to understand where the market is in the real estate cycle in order to position for the best negotiation. Are vacancies rising or falling? What is the trend with landlord concessions? Are effective rent averages moving up, down, or holding steady in your submarket? Most commercial real estate advisors' proprietary databases provide access to these and other lease comparables, to help answer these questions and provide you an edge in the negotiation process.

Step 6 —Commit to an Option

During this phase, you typically negotiate back and forth through responses to the landlord's proposal. The goal is to secure your top property with the very best terms possible through an executed lease, and begin the tenant improvement process immediately.

Once the details of the negotiation are finalized, both parties will either sign a letter of intent (LOI) or move straight into reviewing a draft formal lease. The LOI document is generally non-binding. It presents a good faith representation of the agreed terms and conditions to be embodied in the formal lease document. Once executed, both parties will use LOI document as a foundation to develop the final lease documents. I have seen it work both ways. Sometimes, it is more efficient to just move right to developing the lease document and skip the LOI.

When the formal lease agreement is complete, the tenant improvement process should begin immediately. At this point, your landlord's designer and space planner should be coordinating with the contractor and equipment vendor's technicians for design and installation of all required improvements immediately, as time is of the essence.

Step 7—Design and Project Management

The final stage of the process, prior to occupancy, requires detailed planning and project management. It now is critical to engage and fully brief all team members and consultants with a role in the build-out and move-in. The detailed design should be completed, as tenant improvement costs are finalized at this point. The general contractor should provide you with a detailed construction timeline and periodic progress updates through design and construction. You also need to appoint a project manager to coordinate the logistics related to your facility move and also oversee any tenant improvements that are not being managed by the landlord.

Key Takeaways :

- Know the specific differences between full-service gross leases, modified gross leases, and net leases.
- Most leases have slight variations from standard industry language. It's important to clarify your responsibilities specifically.
- The longer the term, the more valuable the lease to the landlord.
- Review all your options, and assess the current market conditions to understand the overall opportunity for relocation.
- Consider 'blend and extend' if staying in your current facility is an option.
- A well-prepared lease requirement summary clearly defines needs and distills them into the property requirements.

Chapter 7:
Own – Buy Versus Develop

"There are no secrets to success.
It is the result of preparation, hard work,
and learning from failure." - *Colin Powell*

Buy Versus Develop

Once you've decided that it is more advantageous to own than to lease, you have reached another decision point. Should you buy an existing facility or develop a new one from the ground up? Sometimes, the decision is made for you because you have a unique requirement in a market that has no available supply of facilities meeting your needs. If so, you should begin the process of working toward your new facility a minimum of twenty-four months out. More time than that will be needed if you have not already acquired entitled land for the development.

Take the case of Bill Rogers, an entrepreneur who has been growing his industrial remanufacturing business for eight years. Bill has always leased, and his next lease renewal was coming up in twenty-four months. He knew he needed to expand again, and he was also planning for his retirement in the next ten years.

Bill decided that, rather than continuing to lease, he would either purchase or develop, and he knew he needed to get started early. Unfortunately, his particular submarket had limited availability of properties that might, with some modifications, meet his needs. The challenge for Bill was that the cost for the available buildings at the time was averaging over $120 per square foot. Through some investigation and pricing exercises, we determined Bill could construct a new facility, designed to his specific needs in the exact location he desired, for less than $75 per square foot. I'm sure you know which option Bill chose to pursue.

Preparing for and executing commercial real estate acquisitions and developments can be a complex and challenging undertaking even for experts. Business owners' objectives will vary, but long-term goals typically focus on maximizing wealth. Managing these transactions can be a major distraction for entrepreneurs and business executives whose areas of expertise are in different industries.

In the next two chapters, we will cover key considerations for purchasing existing facilities and building / developing to meet your exact specifications. Each option has its own unique set of challenges and risks. However, with proper analysis and strategy, those risks can be managed, and your industrial facility can be leveraged as a tool to move you toward your long-term wealth goals.

Key Takeaways:

- Give yourself plenty of time to analyze buy vs. develop options; ideally begin the process at least 24 months out from the projected need
- Remember that market conditions and business objectives will change over time; leave some flexibility in your plan so you can adjust if necessary

Chapter 8:
Buy an Existing Facility

"Real estate cannot be lost or stolen, nor can it be carried away.
Purchased with common sense, paid for in full, and managed
with reasonable care, it is about the safest investment
in the world." - FRANKLIN D. ROOSEVELT

Why should you consider purchasing existing industrial real estate? There are many strategic considerations. One of the main benefits is to gain more control over your cost of occupancy. In the lease versus buy chapter, we discussed the concept that you can lose big if your lease renewal occurs during an expansionary phase in the market and, as a result, your rental expense escalates. Some of the other main strategic benefits of ownership we covered were the investment components, including depreciation of the property for tax purposes and appreciation of the asset over the longer term.

While no one has a crystal ball, good planning and consideration of important strategic factors can be a profit multiplier for your business. There is no one-size-fits-all strategy for purchasing an industrial

STEPS TO **PURCHASING**

1 Assemble advisory team

2 Develop your needs analysis

3 Conduct market research

4 Tour available space / conduct space planning

5 Prepare letters of intent

6 Negotiate contingent purchase agreement

7 Conduct due diligence

8 Closing and title transfer

9 Execute occupancy plan

property. The analysis and decision must be conducted on a case-by-case basis for each unique situation. After you have examined your strategy and decided to move forward with purchasing an existing facility, it is critical to develop a plan and assemble the resources to enable you to execute. The adjacent graphic illustrates the major steps in the purchasing process, which should be followed in order to achieve your desired outcome.

When it comes to helping business owners achieve their desired outcome with real estate acquisition, there is no one quite like my colleague Jan Boltres. As a 26-year veteran of the industrial real estate industry, Jan has worked as a broker and consultant and advised clients in the acquisition of industrial real estate totaling in excess of $500 million.

During an interview with Jan on this topic, he shared some valuable insights with me on the acquisition process, and he's letting me share them with you here. I wanted to know what tips and guidance Jan could provide to industrial users looking to acquire a space or thinking about the process of acquisition. Specifically, I asked Jan what's important to a business owner who doesn't want to lease but rather wants to buy. What is the next step?

Jan: *It's important to define the long term need. While your immediate need may be very specific, acquiring a building that only meets those very specific needs is not always the best route. For example, it doesn't always allow for an exit strategy.*

If you need 14-foot ceilings, well that's great, nobody else does. It will be difficult to sell that space in the future, after your business plan has run its course. Do not acquire a building that has that functional obsolescence; even though it may work for you now, you're going to pay for it in the long run. Your exit strategy for a building like that is going to be terrible, you're going to get less for it than a comparable building with functional clear height, and it'll take you much, much longer to eventually sell the property.

What are the hot buttons? What makes for a marketable building now, and what do we anticipate will be marketable five, or even ten, years into the future? For example, you may look for a building with some extra land for expansion that somebody else didn't already max out. Expansion options are always worth something down the road. In my career, I have seen examples where the opposite has occurred — where a business acquired an existing building and retrofitted it to meet their immediate needs. Because this was an 80,000 square foot building that used to be 40,000 square feet, and a lot of the parking and loading were sacrificed for the expansion, they now have a building with inferior parking and loading. There is no expansion capability, and all because they took over somebody else's problem.

Q: Do you see a lot of situations in which business owners go out and try to do all this on their own?

Jan: *All the time, and for the life of me, I just don't get it. If you have a successful business, why would you spend your time away from your core business, out doing something that you can have someone far more qualified do for you for free? Is your time that invaluable that you can afford to do that?*

Q: What do you mean by 'free'?

Jan: *There's a commission built in to every deal, lease or sale. The owner, or landlord, is going to pay that fee, not the guy acquiring the building, or not the person leasing the space. You're not saving money by not having a broker, because there is already a fee built in. Do you go to court without an attorney, because you want to save legal fees? Seek the advice of a professional.*

Q: Can business owners find acquisition information for industrial properties on the Internet?

Jan: *They certainly can, but they still need to understand what they're seeing. Some of those buildings have been on the*

market for years, and should be redeveloped or torn down.
An informed broker not only knows the state of the buildings,
but also knows of buildings that aren't on the market, or ones
that are soon to come on the market. The Internet is not a
comprehensive source for commercial real estate information.

Q: So, Jan, thinking about all the users across the country that
may be looking to expand or consolidate their facilities over
the next five or ten years, can you give them any advice or tips
in terms of their acquisition strategies?

Jan: *I would say give more consideration to the possibilities of*
expansion and contraction. Businesses are usually overly par-
anoid about it, committing to short-term leases instead of tak-
ing economic advantage of a long-term lease without explor-
ing expansion and early termination options. When you sign a
two-year lease, you pay a high economic price for that shorter
term. If you renew it again, you get much higher annual rent
increases than you otherwise would in a long-term lease with
an early termination option.

Why not look at the possibilities of a landlord with multiple
parks, buildings, and facilities that could accommodate fu-
ture expansion, would let you out of your obligation to move
or build with them, or has the development capabilities to

allow for other future expansion? The same holds true for contraction. A landlord with multiple properties can offer you those options.

The same is also true from a purchase standpoint. Are you buying a building that does not have expansion capabilities? Are you buying a white elephant building, one that gives your exit strategy a protracted time frame that may prohibit you from acquiring another building because you can't sell the white elephant you bought? These are all things to consider.

Assemble Your Advisory Team

As a business owner and executive, you're most likely not a commercial real estate expert. You're also extremely busy running and growing your business. That's why it is critical to surround yourself with a team of experts that has your best interest in mind. Your team will help you determine the right time to buy or sell, identify important pitfalls, critical negotiating points, and the crucial details of closing the deal. Here is a potential list of experts you should consider adding to your acquisition team:

Commercial Real Estate Attorney—It is critical to find an attorney who specializes in commercial real estate transactions. These professionals deal with the specifics of commercial real estate legal issues on a daily basis and will help you avoid potentially catastrophic pitfalls during acquisition.

Accountant—Your accountant is a key part of your team for several reasons. A good accountant understands your business. He or she will help you figure out what the company can afford and analyze the tax and operating budget implications of ownership on your balance sheet, cash flow, and profit and loss statement.

Mortgage Broker—If you have a pre-existing relationship with a preferred lender, that's great. However, you may benefit by connecting with a mortgage brokerage that specializes in commercial real estate financing. They will help you sort through financing options, including bank loans, small business lending programs like those guaranteed by the U.S. Small Business Administration, and Commercial Mortgage-Backed Security (CMBS) lending.

Commercial Real Estate Broker—Your broker advisor will act as your subject-matter expert in the property type you are pursuing. Choose a broker who will work as a true advisor, one who will understand your business plan and how acquisition of this commercial property supports that plan. Your broker should oversee the acquisition process, acting as your project manager and advisor throughout all phases of execution. Look for a broker representative with excellent market knowledge, extensive experience with the space acquisition process, and strong negotiation skills in order to achieve the best result with your initiative.

General Contractor—In some cases, it is helpful to have a preferred contractor on your advisory team. A helpful contractor should be willing to walk a site with you during the due diligence phase, and help you understand options for retrofitting, renovation, and additional construction costs that might be required for your company to utilize the space.

Develop Your Needs Analysis

You need to define your target and develop your High Value Target (HVT) List. This is where you pull together your key advisors to form your steering committee. For smaller, closely held businesses, this could be just a few key employees and officers. For large or publicly traded companies, this is likely to include more than one committee, with cross-departmental or divisional representation. In any case, it is important the committee be led by a senior employee capable of driving the acquisition project from start to finish. Chances are that person is you. Make sure you include all stakeholders able to impact discussion and decisions in a meaningful way.

Involve key internal stakeholders from the start. Departments that you may not have thought of, such as human resources and finance, can add valuable input and help influence your requirements definition and decisions. Their involvement from the beginning will ensure you develop a comprehensive needs analysis and achieve internal buy-in.

Work with your operations managers, engineers, and plant maintenance to develop your plan based on the best information.

While your HVT list is largely inclusive of operational requirements, it is equally important to consider strategic implications. Consider medium- to long-range goals for your company and how your facility plan will move you toward achieving those goals. Think about including key staff members, your real estate advisor, CPA, and attorney in all or part of the discussions to solicit their input.

Some of the discussion topics should include:
- Your growth plan over the next five to ten years
- Your projected facility needs to support your growth plan (geographic, functional, capacity, size)
- Your corporate values/image and how your facility can/ should support them
- Your exit strategy from the company
- How acquiring property impact your financials (cash flow, balance sheet)
- Impacts if you do not acquire the property
- Potential acquisitions or mergers with other firms
- The impact on transportation and logistics costs
- The impact on suppliers, customers, and staff
- Tax impacts (economic incentives, municipal tax changes, depreciation, and other implications)

By working through these and other topics early in the needs analysis, you will avoid costly mistakes down the road. Once you have gathered input and distilled your needs into a summary of requirements, it is time to develop your market requirement summary.

Your summary will also create a mechanism for evaluating and comparing your options. Begin by defining what is and is not working in your existing facility. Include those components that you believe are important in your summary. Some of the standard criteria we normally include in our requirements summaries are:

- Size of facility
- Percentage of office, warehouse, manufacturing space
- Utility requirements (natural gas, power, water, and data requirements)
- Size of workforce (maximum and minimum)
- Image/quality/aesthetics
- Truck court layout and radius
- Parking requirement (cars and trucks)
- Fire suppression systems
- HVAC
- Ceiling clear height
- Loading doors (type and number)
- Proximity to transportation networks
- Operating hours
- Zoning/allowable impact on intended use

- Security and access

- Lease structure preferences

- Technical requirements

- Budget

- Local incentives

I recommend constructing a comparison matrix that ranks each factor in terms of importance, as you may have to compromise on some items, depending on the options available. You can also assign a point value to each factor, with more points attributed to the factors with greater importance. The matrix template at www.warehouseveteran.com provides a good starting point for the process. Your commercial real estate advisor is also a good resource to guide you through the evaluation process. He or she should provide expertise and experience in the evaluation and decision-making process, as well as bring the specifics of local market knowledge into the equation.

Conduct Market Research

During this phase, it is important to research and understand local market conditions and pricing. By knowing the market and submarket property values, inventory projections, and current vacancy rates, you will be in a better position to evaluate available properties and ultimately negotiate the very best purchase agreement for your company.

Your commercial real estate advisor can provide you with a market presentation that describes these factors in your local market and in specific submarkets you identify as most desirable.

Begin the initial search for space well in advance of when you will need it. If you don't, you may find yourself at a negotiating disadvantage because your needs will be driven by timing, rather than what is the best value for your company. Lean on your advisors to help you understand the amount of time similar searches and transactions are taking in your market. This will help with back planning and ensure that you begin your research and search efforts with enough time allotted to put you at an advantage.

At this point, you should release your requirement summary to the market and begin identifying available options. There are also several commercial real estate marketing databases that are a source of properties available for lease, including CoStar, LoopNet, and Xceligent. To avoid dealing with multiple agents and owners, request that your real estate broker approach the market on your behalf.

Have your advisor match your criteria against all available properties in your market. Additionally, a good broker will know about off-market properties that are to be available soon. To take it one step further, if you have identified specific properties in a target location, you or your broker can contact owners of off-market properties directly, to see if they have an interest in selling. Once you have assembled your list of potential properties from your market survey, have your broker gather specific information on each property to drop into your decision matrix.

Assign a weight to each of the decision criteria that you choose to include in your needs analysis. Evaluate options against your criteria, assigning a score for each measurable item. The goal here is to ensure that you are matching each property's benefits to your weighted evaluation criteria. Once you have scored each property in each category, multiply the score times the weight and summarize the score for each alternative at the bottom of the sheet. Consider eliminating your lowest scoring properties from consideration at this point. Your decision matrix will provide a numerical value allowing a comparison of the pros and cons of the properties, but this is just the start. Next, have your broker representative set up tours for the properties remaining on the target list.

Tour Available Space and Conduct Space Planning

It is time to physically view the available properties that meet your criteria from the market survey. Prior to your visits, you should put together a comprehensive tour package. Try to tour them all within a day or two of each other so you can reasonably compare your impressions of each.

Your broker can set up all of the tours. The broker should prepare a tour book that includes a map, photos, and specifics of each property you will visit. Additionally, I recommend including a comparison matrix in the package so you can rate and compare the potential properties side by side as you are viewing them.

WAREHOUSE VETERAN ACQUISITION ANALYSIS
SAMPLE COMPARISON MATRIX

TOP FIVE CRITERIA	Weight on Scale of 1-10	2446 50th Street	2446 Carrilon Ave	4654 N 35th St
1. Transportation Access	7	9	6	10
2. Proximity to Port	9	9	7	8
3. Outside Storage	5	3	9	2
4. Image	4	5	7	7
5. Cost	4	6	7	2
		203	206	188

A sample of an industrial facility acquisition comparison matrix can be downloaded at www.warehouseveteran.com. So many times, we see people touring all day long and then attempting to compare based on memory after the fact. It is much more effective to define your decision criteria upfront, utilizing your requirements summary, and rate each property for each of the categories as you visit the sites.

After completing the tours, review your notes and, based on comparisons of the properties, eliminate those that no longer make the cut. It's time to begin making decisions. You may want to engage your space planner, architect, and/or general contractor at this point to get a better understanding of the costs, time, and effort required to bring each potential site up to your required configuration and condition. This information should be factored into any offers you make.

Also, at this stage, your commercial real estate broker should provide you a package to help facilitate the best negotiation in your favor. You will need to understand recent comparable sales and competing availabilities, as well as current market factors and the way they are trending. Are prices moving up or down? Which way is vacancy headed in the submarket you are interested in?

You also need to understand as much as possible about the seller's situation. This can help guide your negotiation strategy. What is the "back story" with the property? Why is the owner selling? Is there remaining debt on the property? What is your assessment of the owner's motivation level? Is there interest from other buyers? The more you can complete the puzzle, the bigger advantage you'll score when negotiating price and contract terms.

Prepare Letter of Intent

You have narrowed down your target list to a primary and secondary acquisition targets. It's now time to prepare and issue a letter of intent (LOI). In its most basic form, a letter of intent outlines the important terms and conditions of your proposed acquisition. In most situations, agreement on the basic terms helps facilitate agreement on the remaining terms. A signed LOI is an indication from both parties that a preliminary agreement has been reached on most major components of any potential deal. Regardless of whether you are the seller or the buyer, you and the other party are more likely to feel committed to finalizing a deal when you have formalized a preliminary agreement.

An LOI is a signal to the seller that a qualified buyer is serious about acquiring the property. It is typically not a legally binding document.

To ensure that a LOI is not construed as an enforceable contract, I insert language similar to the following: "This Letter of Intent is not intended to be a legally binding Contract for Sale and Purchase. Neither party shall be bound or have the obligation to pursue negotiations or any other obligations of any kind unless and until a definitive formal contract is hereafter signed and delivered by the parties. Neither the expenditure of funds by either party or reliance on this Letter of Intent nor part performance of any provisions of this Letter of Intent by either party shall alter the foregoing provisions of this paragraph, and notwithstanding any such expenditure or performance, this Letter of Intent shall, as stated above, not constitute a binding Contract for Sale and Purchase."

Of course, you should consult your legal counsel if you are unsure regarding legality or enforceability of any business document.

Here are the main components of a letter of intent for purchase and sale of real property which you should consider including in your LOI:

Definition of the subject—Include reference to the property, legal description, acreage, square footage of buildings and any real property that you intend to include in your purchase offer.

Economic terms—Besides the purchase price, earnest money and other deposits, a LOI may outline how the transaction is to be financed and whether the buyer or seller pays title insurance, recording fees, survey, and other closing expenses.

Inspection period—Ask for a time period in which to perform due diligence on the property and determine its acceptability. Always include the option of cancelling the purchase agreement, with full refund of any deposits, if the property is not determined acceptable. The length of time varies, depending on numerous factors, including the complexity of the transaction, market conditions, and competition from other buyers or lack thereof.

Closing date—The LOI should specify a closing date. Most of the time, this date is expressed as a certain number of days after the occurrence of a stated event, like the expiration of the inspection period.

Brokers—If real estate brokers are involved in the transaction, something I strongly recommend, the LOI should identify the brokers representing each party and also specify how much and by whom the broker is to be paid upon closing.

Confidentiality—A LOI may require the parties to keep negotiations confidential. Of course, this should not limit you from seeking professional assistance from an advisor, such as an attorney or accountant, or discussions with prospective lenders.

Exclusive opportunity—One option is to request that the seller not negotiate with any other party after execution of the LOI.

Nonbinding provision—Your LOI should state that it is for negotiation purposes only and is not binding on the parties.

Develop and Negotiate the Contract

After agreeing on the terms and conditions of the LOI, both parties will execute the document. Most LOIs provide a set number of days in which the parties have to negotiate the final contract for purchase and sale. Select a target date and push all parties involved to stick to it.

It is no secret that any contract can be written in favor of one party or another. If you have an opportunity to provide the initial draft, I recommend you jump on it. Utilize an initial draft that is written with terms and conditions benefiting your situation. The other side can always negotiate for what is important to them.

The bottom line is, if you don't ask for it, you probably won't get it. So, if you have a chance to ask for everything you want out of the gate, go for it. If you don't already have your "perfect" draft contract developed, ask your trusted commercial real estate attorney or broker for one.

If the seller produces the draft contract, don't sweat it. Just make sure to thoroughly review it and ensure that everything you require is included. Involve your legal counsel in a full review of the purchase and sale agreement. Again, it is absolutely critical to seek out counsel from an attorney specializing in commercial real estate contract law. There are too many specific issues that can pop up in the course of a normal deal, and you may suffer tremendous loss if you rely on the advice of an attorney without transaction-specific experience.

Another option is to suggest utilization of standardized contract language, written to provide neutral language for buyers and sellers. In my home state, the Florida Association of Realtors (FAR) publishes a standardized commercial contract called the FAR CC-4. This simple-form contract is available for download and can be a good starting point for parties without a preferred draft contract in place.

Due Diligence

Once you have secured the property under a binding contract, get to work immediately in performing due diligence on the property. Many sellers convey property on an "as-is" basis, which makes it exceptionally important to systematically inspect everything related to the property and ensure you are getting the deal you signed up for. In the contract, ask for as much time as needed, and make sure your deposit is fully refundable if, in your sole discretion, you find the property unsuitable for its intended use.

Most due diligence periods are between thirty and ninety days. Rarely, an owner will allow a longer inspection period, but you have to realize this is where the parties may have conflicting interests. The seller wants to close the transaction as soon as possible after execution of the contract, while the buyer usually has a reason to stretch out the closing for some period of time. Typically, that time is spent ensuring that everything with the property is in order and all risks have been investigated and either eliminated or mitigated.

Sometimes, it may become necessary to take additional time in order to secure entitlements and permits related to the intended use. Depending on the circumstance, the owner may grant additional time or agree to a contingency based on issuance of a zoning approval, special use, or some other required condition. Just remember, everything is negotiable as long as you are still in the due diligence phase of the contract. Timing is important here because you will lose leverage once your deposit becomes non-refundable.

To ensure that you do not miss any important details, I recommend utilizing a due diligence checklist during this process. Due diligence checklists have been around in various forms for as long as I can remember. They provide a simple framework to help you make sure you're not buying someone else's problem.

> Due diligence checklists provide a simple framework to help you make sure you're not buying someone else's problem .

Now, I'm a former military guy, so as a matter of good process, I don't do anything important without a checklist. I can recall several war stories in which the buyer inadvertently skipped a step in the process and ulti-mately was stuck with a building they couldn't use or couldn't sell later.

Mistakes may be as blatant as the building supply company that failed to conduct a Phase I environmental study and purchased a build-ing constructed over a former landfill with contaminated soil. Another was a trucking company that purchased a site, only to learn later they could not park their trucks there because of specific restrictions over-looked in the original development agreement.

Due diligence in commercial real estate (CRE) acquisition starts with the contract negotiations. Ask for ample time in your LOI. Do your best to build in a buffer that gives you the time you need. I recommend negotiating the longest period of time possible; you can always close early once you have completed the process. Also, make sure to prepare a list of key contract dates, communicate them to your team, and track them in your calendar.

The goal is to leave no stone unturned. Beyond the physical condi-tion of the building and the site, there are many intangibles to consider. Literally *every* document concerning the building and its operation *must* be examined. This includes any existing leases with any and all extensions, title policy exceptions, insurance policies, maintenance contracts, environmental reports, survey, zoning restrictions, operating records, building plans, and many others.

Using the list generated for the purchase, I recommend going over each item and assigning it as a task to a member of the acquisition team, whether it's your lawyer, surveyor, building inspector, environmental firm, or yourself. Make sure each team member is contacted and given the timetable for the deal, then follow-up on a very regular basis. Do not skimp on these details. Be sure the list is complete prior to the conclusion of the inspection period. It could easily save you millions.

If any problems are found during the due diligence process, you may be able to renegotiate with the seller or, at the very least, have your deposit refunded and walk away from the deal.

IMPORTANT: Visit warehouseveteran.com to download a sample of the due diligence checklist.

The Million Dollar Mistake

Regardless of what you're developing or purchasing, whether it's a 5,000-square-foot building or a million-square-foot distribution center, you need a defined process for checks and balances to manage due diligence and ensure you're not leaving out any steps through acquisition, design, and construction. Your process must mitigate as much risk as possible by following a known pattern for success in the development of that site. Here is a great example, shared with me by a colleague, of what can happen if you don't perform proper due diligence and quality control throughout the entire acquisition and development process.

A contractor was hired by a principal with one of the nation's largest private development firms to develop a 100,000 square foot big box home improvement facility. The contractor was directed to bring a certain amount of fill material in from a location nearby, which the client had purchased. The material was brought in, the building pad was compacted, concrete was poured over the building pad, and the entire store was constructed. Racking was installed inside, and inventory was about to be brought in, when an issue with the underlying soil was discovered—the foundation wasn't stable.

The developer had failed to conduct quality control and check the soil characteristics of the fill material to ensure it was suitable and free of contaminants. Unfortunately, everything had to be removed from the entire facility, the concrete slab had to be demolished, and all the underlying material dug out and shipped to another location for remediation.

While the building shell did remain in place, the entire interior portion of the building had to be constructed over again from scratch. It ended up costing the developer more than a million dollars, which was a substantial cost, impacting the developer's bottom line.

As a developer or owner, it is your responsibility to make sure someone is checking off all the boxes in the process. In this case, the contractor who brought in the dirt, and then later had to take it out and replace it, got paid three times for the same result. This was a hard lesson for the developer, and it is exactly this sort of scenario that you want to avoid by making sure you have performed your due diligence.

Financing Options

Once you've found the right property and negotiated terms and conditions, you will need to secure financing based on the amount of cash you plan to put in as well as how much you will need to borrow. As an industrial space buyer, you fall into one of three categories: an investor—you plan on renting out the space, an owner/occupant—you will utilize the building for your own operations, or an owner/investor—you will occupy part of the building and the balance will be leased to other tenants. Financing options for owner/occupants and owner/investors differ significantly from those offered the straight investor. For the owner/occupant and owner/investors, the following are the four main sources of debt financing.

Conventional financing

Conventional financing typically offers the most competitive rates for owner-occupied properties. Traditional bank lenders approach the approval process on a more conservative basis than most other lender options. Banks tend to focus on the borrower's underlying financial strength and ability to repay, rather than the financial performance of the business and the property itself. Traditional financing definitely has its advantages. In addition to lower rates than other sources of debt, some banks can lend out to twenty-five-year terms, and most will allow up to twenty-five-year loan amortizations. Also, most conventional financing includes balloon and non-balloon payment options, as well as flexible prepayment options.

Seller financing

Depending on the seller's situation, seller financing may be an option to meet some or all of your financing requirements. I tend to see more seller financing occur during periods with higher interest rates and less availability of credit. Under those circumstances, sellers must get creative and find ways to sell property in the absence of abundant buyer financing options. The advantages of seller financing is avoidance of certain transaction fees associated with traditional and SBA lending, such as appraisal fees and expensive origination fees. Seller financing is also much easier to qualify for and is typically applied as non-recourse debt. The main disadvantage is a higher rate associated with borrowing directly from the seller.

Third-party financing

Borrowing from a friend or relative willing to make an investment in your business may provide a nice investment alternative to someone who has stockpiled cash in a savings account or money market. The personal lender can earn a higher return through an investment that is collateralized by commercial real estate.

There are also scores of private lenders willing to lend to owner/occupant and owner/investors. While you might win big with a lower rate and superior loan terms by financing with a friend or relative, using a third-party finance company has its advantages. They typically offer both recourse and non-recourse lending options, and approvals are based on the strength of the underlying asset's performance versus the financial strength and guarantee of the principals. Disadvantages of private lending options include higher rates and less flexibility in pre-payment penalties.

SBA loans

Created in 1953 as an independent agency of the federal government, the stated mission of the U.S. Small Business Administration (SBA) is to aid, counsel, assist and protect the interests of small business concerns, to preserve free competitive enterprise, and to maintain and strengthen the overall economy of our nation. The SBA offers real estate loan guarantees through one of two types of loans: a 504 or 7A loan. The 504 loan is a 50 percent first loan from a bank and a 40 percent second loan from the government. The 7A loan is a 90 percent government-guaranteed bank loan.

These loans have their advantages and disadvantages. The advantages of both loans include small down payments such as 10 percent, fixed interest rates, the ability to finance building improvements, and wide availability from a number of lending sources. The disadvantages of both are the origination fees, the prepayment penalties, the collateral and personal guarantees, and the business requirements of profitability and number of years in business. Most advisors will tell you that, if you don't absolutely need an SBA guarantee, you don't want one. If you chose to pursue this option, be aware that the SBA will require you to pledge every asset you have to your name to collateralize the loan. When they say "every asset," they mean it—including your 401k, IRA, and key man life insurance. And more than likely, this option will require a mortgage on your house.

Key Takeaways:

- Do not rely on the internet as a comprehensive source of information for commercial real estate acquisition
- Leverage your advisory team to save you time and provide key information to ensure success during the acquisition process
- Following a disciplined approach to the acquisition process will ensure that you meet both your long and short term property goals plus avoid all major pitfalls
- Pay particular attention to detail during the due diligence process to avoid getting stuck with someone else's problems

Chapter 9:
Develop New Facility – Site Selection & Programming

"Plan for what is difficult while it is easy,
do what is great while it is small." – SUN TZU

You have performed your analysis and are thinking about developing your own industrial facility. You've decided it makes sense when compared to options like acquiring an existing building, and you have weighed the costs against all other strategic implications that will affect your business. Now what? You will need to develop your conceptual design and select potential sites to begin focusing on your timing and cost.

Project Considerations

Start with the end in mind. What will the final outcome look like? Spending extra time upfront to really understand your goals and objectives pays big dividends down the road. You have a blank slate, and this is your chance to develop a masterpiece that will become a profit multiplier for your business. It is very important to solicit input from key advisors early on, including operations, logistics input, trusted vendors, engineers, contractors, and an architect.

Start the selection process by thinking about location. Most businesses utilizing industrial space want to locate facilities as close as possible to the core customer base. Obviously there are anomalies to this rule, but most companies will want to move closer to their customers, not farther away, as we are experiencing realignment of supply chains to keep up with the changing shape of how goods flow from manufacturers and distributors to end-users.

Next, decide whether you need a stand-alone warehouse to serve national or regional demand, or if your objective is to complement an existing distribution network with the addition of a new building or replacement of another building. A company with one warehouse in Los Angeles, for example, would not locate another warehouse in Phoenix to serve national demand. It would choose an East coast city, or perhaps Atlanta or Chattanooga. If you haven't already analyzed your current and projected flow of goods and overlaid it with your strategic facility plan, this is the time to do so. There are many consultants and logistics-modeling firms to assist if this is a topic that will affect your specific situation.

Most of my best clients tell me they base their location decisions on a combination of customer service requirements and cost objectives. Other overall objectives may include:

- Designing a delivery network that provides competitive advantage.
- Providing a flexible and rapid response distribution network.
- Minimizing operating costs while still preserving quality and service capability.

The goal should include developing your supply network with the intention of minimizing transportation costs, while still delivering to a specified service standard. One example would be to develop a network with the lowest possible distribution cost that still allows for delivery to 80 percent of the customer base utilizing two-day ground shipping.

Top Five Most Common Factors in Industrial Site Selection

Decision-making for industrial facility site selection can be challenging. The outcome is, without a doubt, critical to the success of future operations. In most cases, it will have a major impact on the success or failure of your enterprise. There are five critical success factors that most commonly dominate the site selection process for the businesses we work with. The following summary is offered with the local or regional manufacturing or distribution business in mind. Each situation will vary, and most businesses have different criteria, depending on their unique strategies, products, and mission. The important takeaway is to determine your top factors in evaluating potential sites and use them to guide your decision-making process using the site selection matrix provided as a free tool on our website at www.warehouseveteran.com.

Site Selection Factor #1: Supplier/Market Connection

While quick highway access in and out of your facility is important to your location, proximity to your current or future suppliers and customers is critical. If your business experiences a cost impact related to inbound or outbound shipments, consider investing in simulation modeling and network optimization exercises to deliver meaningful information for consideration in your site selection process. Think about the current (and projected) shipping locations of your suppliers, as well as the delivery locations for your key customers. Where is most of your output shipped? Is the site positioned in the best location to minimize overall transportation costs? Of course, if you import or export raw materials or finished product, you must also consider locations with close access to intermodal facilities.

Critical Site Selection Factor #2: Availability of Skilled Labor

In dealing with many different businesses across various industries, I have found that growing companies are usually more worried about adequately fulfilling demand than generating it. At the time of writing this book, economic expansion and a growing resurgence of manufacturing in the U.S. are driving an increased demand for skilled labor in most primary and some secondary markets across the country. Access to an available, skilled labor force is a critical success factor for most businesses that utilize industrial space. If you fall in this category, it is important to understand current and projected labor pool availability for the geographic markets and submarkets you are considering. Additionally, make sure to understand the implications of operating in a right-to-work state, as more and more companies will not consider working in a state that is not based on right-to-work law.

States and municipalities competing for jobs are responding to this need more than ever. Most regions competing for new and expanding businesses are engaged in comprehensive labor force training programs. These programs are normally funded at the state level and provide training at no charge for many expansions and new operations, primarily through the state technical college systems. Some programs also contract with private industrial trainers to provide supplementary efforts. For more information, contact your state or local economic development agencies. A skilled commercial real estate advisor should be your ally and a helpful resource in providing local labor data, as well as contacts to local sources of skilled labor and training programs.

Site Selection Factor #3:
Land/Construction Cost

Land costs are an important consideration depending on your intended market or submarket. Industrial land surrounding more active primary and secondary metropolitan areas commands higher prices than rural or tertiary markets, where land is less of a cost factor.

While land prices will rise and fall depending on supply and demand factors, costs for new construction and improvements to existing facilities are driven by other factors. These include the availability and cost of raw materials, availability of local labor pools, cost of capital for financing, site-specific requirements, and local contractor availability. We advise our clients to connect with one or two reputable general contractors in advance of developing a new site or purchasing an existing site that will require improvements. This relationship can serve as a foundation for future cost estimates and construction advice. In return, the contractor should expect an opportunity to work on, or at least bid on, your future project.

It is important to have a good grip on cost impacts between different locations due to site-specific requirements. For example, if you are considering a low elevation site that may require imported fill for the building pad and parking lots, a critical part of the decision making process will include understanding how much import fill is required to balance the site, and how much that import material will affect the cost of the project. I have worked on large site projects that have required over 400,000 cubic yards of fill dirt. Considering that the cost exceeded $10 per cubic yard to deliver, spread, and compact, it was a major cost component of the overall project.

Site Selection Factor #4: State & Local Incentives

Economic development incentives at the state and local level are meant to encourage development in a specific geographic location. Targeted programs crafted to attract or retain businesses, usually with financial assistance or tax relief, can offer the business owner the possibility of a quick payoff.

If you are thinking about moving your business to a new space, opening a new facility, or adding a new division with significant new hires, start the incentive application process before your plans are finalized. As a general rule, economic incentives are only provided as a catalyst to influence your decision to locate into a specific region. Therefore, in order to qualify, it is critical to apply for these potential benefits before you make any decisions. Expanding a plant or hiring new workers might earn you tax credits for the new hires, or qualify you for training money, or provide tax relief for material and equipment purchases.

It is important to keep a low profile throughout the process. In some cases, you may want to seek out and apply for benefits anonymously, if possible, before publicly announcing plans to move to a new location or build a new facility, with the goal of avoiding industry rumors with competitors and layoff concerns internally among employees. Another concern is that you can potentially void any incentives if the state or municipality finds out it has been selected as your new location prior to finalization of the incentive package.

Most small and medium sized businesses lack the resources to research, apply for, and pursue available tax credits and incentives, particularly if they are focused on their current operations while simultaneously moving to or opening a new facility, hiring new employees, and other business related tasks. To address these competing requirements, assign a project leader to be responsible for credits and incentives long before investing in facility space or new jobs. If your business doesn't have the resources internally, there are many consultants who specialize in advising businesses on maximization of available incentives.

Keep in mind that incentive packages usually include local employment commitments that your business must deliver over a multiple year timeframe. Make sure that you allocate resources to tracking and reporting any required benchmarks in order to avoid violations or penalties as a result of the incentive agreement.

Site Selection Factor #5: Tax

When considering tax implications of site selection, take a close look at the broad array of taxes that will impact both your business and its employees, including personal income taxes, sales and use taxes, tangible taxes, property taxes, local business taxes, and state corporate tax rates. Recently, many states have enacted packages that include substantial cuts in, or restructuring of, these types of taxes. Some localities are more business-friendly than others, and it is important you understand the tax effects associated with locating at your potential new site.

It is also important to consider that relocation incentives are helpful at the time of relocation, but the tax rate will be there for the long term. A number of states and municipalities are now moving to revise their tax structures with a focus on attracting business and jobs for the long haul without incentives. Other states are moving toward a single sales tax or an apportionment for income tax. Eventually, the states that haven't adapted their tax structures to remain competitive will lose out in the competition for relocating business and jobs.

Site Selection Decision Making Matrix Tool

To compare and contrast best alternatives, develop a decision matrix that ranks your top five to ten site selection criteria with a weight—between one and five is a good range. Next, rate your top site choices side by side, assigning a score to each—usually between one and ten. Finally, multiply the score by the weight for each site selection factor under each comparable site to come up with a numeric value. While this is not a perfect system, it provides an objective reference to aid you and your team in the decision making process.

Layout Considerations

Choose your design team carefully, and interview design consultants with industrial layout and design experience. These architects and consultants will assist you in designing the facility around your strategic requirements.

Collecting operations data is often the first step in this process. Utilizing historical, and projected data is the most important source of input in designing the size and layout of your facility. From that information, you can model facility throughput based on daily shipping and receiving activity. Projecting future inventory levels is the most difficult and critical task associated with sizing and designing a facility to provide future functionality and required capacity. Inventory is the major space driver in most distribution facilities. It is critical that you get it right. A 25 percent deviation on a 100,000-square-foot warehouse would result in a 25,000-square-foot surplus or shortfall.

Inbound shipment characteristics also play a large role in design. While some inbound shipments consist of full pallet, pre-loaded SKU's, ready to put into inventory, others may require testing, sorting, or bundling before being added to inventory. This means the product must be quarantined in a separate receiving area while it is prepped for the next step in the receiving process. No matter how simplified or complex your receiving process, make sure the facility design accounts for efficiency, scalability, and safety requirements of inbound shipments.

Dock layout and operational requirements are also key design factors. Dock capacity constraints can significantly affect functionality of facility operations. When determining layout, as well as the number of required docks, some things to consider include the quantity and schedule of inbound and outbound shipments, unloading and loading times, the number of different product types, pallet breakdown requirements, and special product handling requirements.

Layout Analysis

Once you work through the details of your layout design with your design consultant, you will most likely be presented with options. Evaluate the design options to ensure they meet your expectations and vision before moving to the next stage with any specific design option. A quick evaluation with your advisor should review ROI, functionality, and practicality. As we suggest with most major facility decisions, consider developing an evaluation matrix that compares the capital and operating cost requirements associated with each layout and facility option.

A detailed analysis of each design possibility should consider both quantitative and qualitative aspects. Your design professional will assist you in this process and guide you toward the option that best fits your strategic and tactical business goals. Some of the components to zero in on at this stage would be:

Product flows—How well does the product move through the facility? Are there design opportunities to improve flow and eliminate bottlenecks or constraints that restrict movement?

Design flexibility—Does the design provide for an adaptable facility that can change with operational requirements?

Manpower—Does the design accommodate the personnel required for operations at peak output? Is there design scalability to account for any potential future automation upgrades?

Mobile equipment—What are the right mobile equipment types and capacities for various functional requirements? Will the equipment handle peak requirements?

Conveying and sorting machinery—Do you have the right layout for required conveying and sorting equipment? Are layouts as functional and efficient as possible for intended use?

Capital budgets—Does your capital budget include allowances for equipment, facility upgrades, and information systems software and hardware?

Annual operating budgets—Have you considered the impact of project staffing, maintenance, and utilities costs for the facility?

Sometimes, after carefully reviewing and analyzing design options, two or more designs may appear equally matched. One way to test the efficiency of each is through computer modeling. Your layout consultant can advise you on this. The models will illustrate a typical day's activity in the warehouse. They can simulate peak activity, or run simulations that show the effect of breakdowns or material shortages to reveal weak spots in a particular design. Feedback from my clients indicates that computer models often help one design emerge over the other competing designs.

Functional Layout

I recommend my clients spend a good deal of effort on functional layout, because it affects the nuts and bolts of your business, your daily operational throughput, the cost of production or distribution, and more. Exit strategy considerations are also important. When you're designing a building, understand that, over the life of the building, you give up some value based on how specific the use you design for. For example, if you only require a 14-foot ceiling clear height to operate your assembly process, you should consider increasing the minimum clear height design to at least 24 clear, because a 14-foot clear building is functionally obsolete to most users in today's market. Yes, there will be additional cost to increase the building height, but that cost will be negligible compared to the cost of owning an obsolete building that is difficult to lease or sell when you decide to move on. Designing and constructing a building that allows for a profitable exit should be a key consideration in your functional layout process.

Begin with the End in Mind

When considering buying or developing a facility for a business use, begin with the end in mind. Think about your exit strategy, and how you can best prepare to maximize financial outcome when that time comes.

For example, if part of your succession plan is to sell the business in ten years, think about how to position the building so you'll be able to get the highest and best price in the sale or when leased to another user.

Specific use for your operating business is important, but it's also crucial to remember that, after the space is sold or leased, another party may want a different component in the design.

A popular trend among many of our customers is owning the facility in an LLC or corporate entity that is separate from the core business. This allows you flexibility to scale partnerships within the operating business without having an effect on ownership in the building. Many of our clients look at the investment in their facilities as a separate annuity or portion of their retirement planning. Not only does owning the facility in a separate LLC provide an additional legal barrier for your asset, it also allows you to develop various income streams by leasing the facility to your operating business, which can accommodate many different ownership configurations.

Other Design Considerations

The following list concerns the determination of important physical design requirements from industrial facility users. Consider incorporating this list into any client discovery sessions your designer conducts with you in the design process.

1. What is the optimum ceiling height of the facility?
2. Do you know what the required live floor loads and racking point loads will be in your facility?
3. What is the optimum layout for inbound and outbound shipments, handling, and storage (i.e., double-load, linear dock, cross dock)?
4. What are your specific dock equipment requirements?
5. How many loading doors are required, what will be the dock level and grade level/ramp be, and what dock sizes are optimal?
6. What specific work safety requirements need to be incorporated?
7. Is there a defined specification that includes lighting intensity?
8. What type of facility lighting is preferred?

9. What are the optimum column grids throughout the facility?

10. How many trucks do you expect to have on site at peak times?

11. What are your external physical security requirements (i.e., security cameras, fencing, gate systems, guard huts, etc.)?

12. What are the internal security requirements (i.e., conduits for security system installation including cameras, card readers at specific entrances, etc.)?

13. What are the sprinkler requirements?

14. What type of lift trucks will be used in the facility?

15. What are the specific charging/refueling and maintenance requirements?

16. What is the minimum electrical service requirement for your operations?

17. Do you require cooler, freezer, vaults, FRP paneled rooms or any other specialized product storage spaces within the facility?

18. Do you require any storage outside the facility?

19. Any specific utility, recycling, or refuse disposal requirements?

20. Is a specific communications infrastructure required for the property or within the building?

21. What separate staff facilities are required in the warehouse (i.e., restrooms, showers, locker-rooms, lunch rooms, first aid rooms, etc.)?

22. What are the operational requirements for shipping/receiving offices, driver reception areas, etc., within the facility?

Ultimately, companies build new facilities for a few different reasons: to increase output and efficiency, to reduce operating costs such as production or warehouse operations, and to enhance customer service levels. While the specific layout and functional aspects of each design varies, one fact remains: a thoughtfully designed industrial facility that is well run and efficient will stand out as a profit multiplier to its operator, delivering profitability and scalable capability as its reward.

Key Takeaways

- Start Early and Go Deep – Extra time and effort spent during the planning and programming stage will pay huge dividends upon completion – 36 months is ideal

- Your layout should balance considerations for ROI, functionality, practicality, and building exit strategy

- Use a Site Selection Decision Matrix Tool to compare weighted value scores of candidate sites and help keep the decision making process as objective as possible

Chapter 10:
Develop New Facility
– Getting it Done

"The secret of getting things done is to act!" - DANTE

Selecting and working with
a contractor: GC or CM?

What is the difference between a general contractor (GC) and a construction manager (CM)? There are many similarities, and a couple of differences, the biggest one being the contractual relationship between the owner and the contracting entity.

Under a general contracting relationship, the construction team typically consists of three parties: the owner, the architect, and the general contractor. The GC can either work for an owner under a design-build relationship (where one party is responsible for both the design and construction) or under a design-bid-build relationship. This is where the owner hires a designer to first develop drawings and specifications, which GCs bid on and ultimately construct on behalf of the owner. We will discuss the advantages and disadvantages of these relationships further in the chapter.

Under a CM relationship, the construction manager becomes the fourth member of the team. GCs can act as CMs under specific contractual relationships where they agree to represent the owner under a CM relationship. CMs generally get involved in the project in the early planning stages, providing independent advice and expertise from the beginning to the end of the project. They are responsible for representing the owner's interests in the planning, design, construction, scheduling, and overall management of the project. They typically manage a general contracting firm or a group of specific subcontractors.

Roles of Construction Managers

CMs can operate under different roles when working for an owner. Typically, these are defined under two different types of contractual relationships:

Agency CM—Sometimes, it makes sense to hire an independent professional advisor to manage the project from conception to completion. This role is usually called "Agency CM" (or "CM Advisor" by the American Institute of Architects). Usually, the CM acts solely in the interests of the owner, and the CM's judgment is not influenced by any monetary interest in labor or materials used in the project. It is your CM

Advisor's duty to act in your best interests and advise you in affairs related to the project as you manage your design and construction team. CM Advisor services are usually contracted on a fee-for-services basis.

CM at Risk—This contractual relationship places the project budget risk on the CM, and expands the CM's role. Along with providing professional advice, the CM engages subcontractors on a contractual basis for the purposes of completing the project construction and assumes the responsibilities of delivering the project at a guaranteed maximum price. The risk of completing the project on time, and at a maximum price, effectively makes the CM the contractor as well.

When you compare and contrast, the CM plays a very different role than a typical GC. While the Agency CM does not perform any actual construction or have contractual relationships with subcontractors, the CM at Risk does act as the contractor. The main difference between CM at Risk and GC is that a CM at Risk is involved in the early stages of the entire project, including planning and design. Compare this to a GC in the "traditional" design-bid-build delivery system, who is not involved until the planning and design phase are generally complete.

In my opinion, neither method is better than the other in all cases. The optimal contracting relationship is unique to each situation and the type of project. If you are constructing a very basic, standard project with no unique or challenging characteristics, you will probably be best served to design the project with input and guidance from a couple of trusted GCs, allowing them to bid on the project once your drawings and specifications are complete. If, on the other hand, you have a unique building requirement on a challenging site and short timeframe, hiring an Agency CM or pursuing a CM at Risk relationship with a qualified CM may be the best option.

Project Delivery Method

Whether you choose a traditional GC relationship or you decide a CM is best for your project, you still need to decide whether to utilize design-build or design-bid-build methodology for your project. There are distinct advantages and disadvantages to each.

Design-Bid-Build

Design-bid-build—also known as the "traditional method" or "hard bid method"—is a project delivery method in which the agency CM or owner contracts with separate entities for the design and construction of a project (usually an architect for design and a GC for construction). There are three main sequential phases to the design-bid-build delivery method:

- The design phase
- The bid phase

- The construction phase

Because design and construction are not integrated in this method, it generally takes more time to complete the project. There is less opportunity for schedule consolidation and early site-work startup because the design and specifications must be completed (or close to completion) before the owner or CM can place the project out for bid.

Benefits of Design-Bid-Build

- Competitive selection process for both the design team and contractor improves the opportunity to minimize cost to the owner.
- Assists the owner in establishing budgets in the early stage of development.
- Provides an opportunity for value engineering throughout the design development process.
- Provides an opportunity to vet out design errors during the bid process, through checks and balances and multiple bids from contractors reviewing the same specs and drawings.
- Design team acts as the owner's advocate during the buyout and construction process.

Disadvantages of Design-Bid Build

- Design team can become disconnected with current construction costs in a rapidly changing market.

- Inflation risk during design phase; owner cannot lock in prices until drawings and specs are complete.

- Contracts between the designer and GC are separate; the owner has liability for anything the goes wrong.

- In a hard bid scenario, contractors may compete heavily on price basis and have a tendency to seek out the lowest cost subcontractors. This can result in an increased on-time project completion risk, mostly for the GC, but can also affect quality. It can also create a risk of delay if a subcontractor fails to perform during the project.

- The architect and contractor can have competing interests, which can lead to disputes over quality versus cost, creating project delays and hassles for the owner.

- The owner takes on risk for the design with the GC. If there is a conflict or error in the design, it is on the owner to work it out with the designer. The contractor absorbs no risk for design errors and omissions.

- Construction cannot begin until well after drawings and specs are completed, the project is bid, and a contractor is selected, in contrast with design-build where an early start is possible.

Bottom line, if you decide to develop using design-bid-build, get recommendations for three to five well qualified architects with experience designing industrial facilities. This can, and does, make a difference in the outcome, as there are unique design considerations for industrial assets compared to other types of structures. Make sure to sit down and interview your top two or three candidates in person. Remember, you are going to have to work with this person for the next twelve months at a minimum. Attitude and disposition are equally as important as technical skill. Choosing a design team that understands your vision and respects your business concerns will make all the difference in your satisfaction and the outcome of your project.

> Attitude and disposition are equally as important as technical skill.

If you are working with a CM, lean on them as your advisor as you select the designer and the contractor. I recommend using a best value approach: evaluate the potential team based on multiple weighted factors, with price being just one of the factors. Others you may want to consider are:

- Past Performance—project ratings from previous customers.
- Experience—evaluate experience that is both relevant and recent.
- Schedule—require and evaluate a proposed schedule.
- Quality Control Program
- Safety Record

Design-Build

A design-build contract, as the name implies, combines both the design element and the construction into one single contract. In some cases, the design-build team is based on a joint venture or teaming arrangement between separate general contracting and design firms. In other cases, the design-build firm has its own in-house design and general contracting capability. In almost all cases, the contract between the owner and the design-builder should include a prime contractor. This ensures that, if there is a problem, you are not trying to work with two separate parties pointing fingers at each other. Make sure you have one single point of contact and accountability responsible for your project.

Design Build Advantages

- One point of contact—Design-builders have both parties within the same entity, making it much easier for the owner throughout project development. The owner has only to contact the design-builder about any project questions or concerns.

- Less contractual risk—A single contract, rather than one contract with the design firm and one with a contractor, eliminates the risk of disputes between the parties.

- Fastest delivery method—Eliminating the bidding process and accelerating mobilization saves a significant amount of time. Site preparation can begin prior to the finalization of all building details.

- Less contractual risk—The design-builder is held responsible for design errors and conflicts, eliminating owner liability for design and construction issues.

- Cost control—Design-builders have access to most recent construction costs, and designs are created with the most cost-effective materials and methods.

- Integrated services—Combining both design and construction services eliminates conflicts in most areas of project development. All parties are on the same page, allowing fast-tracked schedules and on-time delivery.

Design Build Disadvantages

- Less advocacy for the owner—The designer is no longer a third party, separate from the contractor, as the design-build team is one and the same.

- Owner has less control and project insight—The designer represents the design-build contractor's best interests rather than the owner's, as in the case of a design-bid-build project.

- Upfront effort—Extensive effort is required upfront to create goals, objectives, and a clear definition of project requirements. A bid package for a design-build project typically includes bridging documents, which are usually 30 percent drawings and limited specs.

In the design-build scenario, you should hire an architect at the very beginning of the project, to prepare design-build criteria documents (also referred to bridging documents). This architect will not ultimately design the entire project; he or she will only create the initial conceptual documents for the bid package. This allows you more input into the conceptual design and your standards for the project.

Due to the uniqueness of industrial space, you also may want to include an industrial layout consultant to provide input on the design. There is always more than one way to incorporate distribution or manufacturing systems into a building's design. Your team should include consultants with specific experience regarding your required systems. They will work closely with your lead designer in the conceptual stage to understand your company's operational needs, preferences, and goals in order to develop a design and technology that optimizes your specific business. They will develop multiple design concepts, with a complete cost-benefit analysis of each. Some of the systems your designer should provide input on include:

- Specific structural, ceiling clear height, and power requirements to address immediate and projected system needs.
- Conveyor system design.
- Manufacturing line layout and design.
- Unique mechanical, electrical, and plumbing design requirement (MEP)
- Maximized efficiency of aisle layout, to gain space and improve warehouse productivity.

- Layout of rack and shelving.

- Use of vertical or horizontal carousels to maximize space.

This approach to constructing industrial facilities is full of details, and Bill Robey knows how to navigate this area like a pro. Bill is a career construction professional, having served in senior executive management roles for several national and global construction services firms over the past 35 years. Bill has ground-up experience across all sizes and scopes of projects, and I caught up with him to secure some solid tips for owners exploring the construction of a new facility. I asked Bill how he would advise anyone interested in developing a new industrial facility, and here's what he had to say:

Bill: *To start with, you've got to take a moment and do a very honest self-assessment of your own in-house capabilities when it comes to managing any development and construction project. There is a lot of detail in any development and construction project, and it is probably a rare individual who has the expertise to singularly manage all of those different elements. So I recommend starting with a very honest assessment of strengths, weaknesses, and capabilities, either as an individual or as an organization, to manage the overall development and construction process.*

Q: Let's say we go through that process, and it's very apparent that we don't have the personnel or the resources to manage the project. What about construction managers? Do you recommend engaging construction managers for that type of development project?

Bill: *Yes, I do. There are three predominant methods of project delivery. You start with the traditional approach of design-bid-build, where you hire the architect and engineer to do a design.*

Once the design is completed, you put that project out for bid to some local qualified contractor pool, and then those contractors provide you proposals. You evaluate these proposals against the plans and specs and you go to contract with the contractor to build. That's the very traditional approach. From start to finish, it's also probably the most linear and lengthy approach to delivering a project. Quite frequently on these types of projects, you will encounter situations with a timeline or race to market requirement as well.

When time is of the essence, start talking about another system, a design-build methodology where you hire a single entity to manage both the design and the construction of the process. And that has some very clear advantages in that it offers you early input into the cost of your project while you're still in design, as well as the ability to shorten that period of time to market. These are really the strengths of the design-build process.

Q: What are the weaknesses of the design-build process?

Bill: *The design-build process is built on trusting relationships and much more open communication. It requires fully engaged and fully committed participants. Some clients I've encountered have felt they did not have the time or the expertise to manage both the design and the construction process so they tended to view design-build as limiting their amount of input into a project. This is a fallacy that is doomed to failure. Design-build does not necessarily have to put any limitations on the owner's involvement in the project.*

Q: What about the cost of development? There's some rumor out there that if you choose the design-build option, you are going to pay more for the ultimate end product. Is that true?

Bill: *No, it isn't. There have been a number of studies done in this case. Before I get into that, let me just briefly describe the third design delivery option. You will hear from time to time about*

CM at-risk wherein you as an owner hire both the architect and the contractor, very similar to the traditional approach, but with CM at-risk, you eliminate the potential weaknesses. You, as the owner, still hire the contractor, you still hire the architect but you integrate the contractor into the design at a much earlier stage where you can get significant and real feedback on cost instead of waiting until the end of the design to find out. You also gain the benefit of fast-tracking the design somewhat in the construction. The time to market is less using that approach, very similar to design-build. It is a hybrid approach between the design-build and the design-bid-build methods of delivery.

Q: Where does the Construction Manager (CM) come into play in that scenario (CM at-risk)?

Bill: *The CM is typically the contractor, working in a more open environment. That process, CM at-risk, also is a very open communication relation-based, trust-based relationship, which is important because they are working right at the shoulder of the owner and the design team very early in the process. They give the team constructability input and significant cost input so that decisions can be made based upon all available information.*

Q: Does the at-risk moniker indicate that the construction manager has a guaranteed maximum price or some other way
he's at risk?

Bill: *Traditionally, the owner still has some risks for the design,
but given the parameters, the idea is to work through the
design process toward a budget based on a performance plan
the contractor can deliver. The end goal is the development
of a guaranteed maximum price that you can move forward
on with the construction manager as the contractor. That's
where the at-risk component in the equation is; the contractor is on board ultimately leading to a guaranteed maximum
price, and now he's at risk to deliver the project at that construction price.*

Q: What do you look for in a construction team if you are going
to develop a project?

Bill: *We talk about doing business-to-business and compa-
ny-to-company, but the reality is that our industry is a people
industry. Like many other businesses, it comes down to the
people and the personnel assigned to a project. So yes, if I'm
looking to develop a project as an owner and developer, I may
interview firms that have a track record in the type of delivery*

*and the type of project that I want to do, but that's not nec-
essarily a guarantee for success either. I would always recommend going one step further and doing your due diligence on
the actual project team. I would get down to the individual
personnel level within a team. All of these processes are built
on a certain level of communications. There should be no sur-
prise communications throughout a project.*

*You are creating a construction 'team' for your project. That
team is going to include architects and engineers as well as
constructors, so it's helpful to understand how all these players have potentially worked together in the past. Look for
proven track records, both for the larger firms and for individual teams of personnel.*

Q: In terms of the actual process, what advice would you offer based on the following scenario: A window manufacturer
has decided to build a 50,000 square foot warehouse. They
have secured the land and now it's time to go out and find a
contractor. They're looking at using a design-build approach.
They interview the different specialists that build warehouses
in their geographic region. They choose one, they go to contract, and now they have hit the timer and the clock starts.
What would you say is important for the owner to consider
when it comes to managing the design, construction, and the

ultimate completion and occupancy of that building? In terms of managing the process around how people are paid, I wanted to know how you make sure you are getting the quality that you're looking for.

Bill: First, have a very clear definition of the program and desired outcome.

This is a crucial first step. It becomes the road map for the entire construction team. It's like the old adage, "If you don't have any plan as to where you want to go, any road will get you there." Having a clear definition of your program to start with is of vital importance.

Second, know what you don't know. *There may be some areas that you don't really have full definition on at that time, but understanding what you don't know is also important. That becomes part of the process for the design and construction team to help you, as the owner, flesh out as you move through the design.*

Third, choose the right team. *Likely, you selected a contractor based on due diligence, past experience and the project team's ability to work together. Understand, especially if you go design-build, that it's a slightly different methodology to the traditional approach. Again, with design-bid-build and* *construction management at-risk, you as the owner will be individually controlling contracts with architects, engineers and construction firms. Under the design-build methodology, part of the streamlining process is for you to have one contract to control, and that's typically with the contractor, who is then going to hire the architects and engineers. There is this perception that you lose some control in that process, but with the right team, right relationship, and open communication, the owner doesn't lose control. What you actually gain is more control of your project delivery schedule.*

One question to ask is: What are the perceived or real benefits on any construction project? The three elements you're always trying to measure are cost, schedule, and quality. Those are the three outcomes that we're looking to maximize.

When I started in this industry, they were still commonly referred to as cost, schedule, and quality. Nowadays, you're more likely to hear this stated as better, cheaper, faster, and in the end, those are the three elements that you're looking to control.

There have been countless studies comparing the various methods of delivery, and time and time again, those studies come back and show that both design-build and CM at-risk deliver very little difference on cost, quality, and overall schedule. Both hold a significant advantage across the board on any three of those measurables to the traditional design-bid then build approach.

Taking Bill's wise advice and experience into consideration, I recommend using a transparent selection process to hire your design build or CM at-risk contractor. Utilize your bridging documents as the basis of your Request for Pro-

Consider experience, past performance, financial qualifications, and scheduling, in addition to price, in evaluating the potential candidates.

posal (RFP). Just as I recommend with the design-bid-build contractor selection, I recommend selecting a design-build contractor based on best value. Price should be only one of the factors in making your selection.

Look at the experience and expertise of the firm, as well as the key personnel on the proposed team, the experience of the team in working together, the technical merits of the design, the project appearance, the contractor's quality and safety programs, references, schedule, and cost. The selection criteria and weighing should be defined in your RFP.

The owner's designer, who prepares the bridging documents, should provide oversight during the final design and construction to represent the owner's interest and help assure everything is completed in conformance with the bridging documents.

I have successfully completed projects under both design-build and design-bid-build methods. Understanding the advantages and disadvantages of each and following a process to address them helps assure the completed project is a success.

Selection methods

There are three traditional methods of contractor selection under both design-build and design-bid-build. (Note: The low-bid method is rarely used with design-build because of the emphasis on quality and process that is required.)

- **Low-bidder or Lowest Price Technically Acceptable (LPTA):** This process focuses almost solely on the lowest qualified price. The idea is to generate a well-defined scope of work and bid it out to multiple qualified GCs or CM firms. If you decide to utilize this method, make sure to prequalify your bidders, provide very well defined drawings and specs, and make sure that your bid sheet includes a bid form so you can compare apples to apples on all of the bids submitted for review.

- **Best Value:** This method focuses on both the price and qualifications of the contractors submitting bids. The owner has an opportunity to choose a contractor based on a combination of factors (other than just price), meaning the owner chooses the contractor with the best price and the best qualifications. Typically, the contractor is selected based on developing and reviewing responses to an RFP. The RFP should be transparent in identifying selection criteria and weighting. Some criteria to consider are: experience and expertise of the firm as well as the key personnel on the proposed team, experience of the team working together, technical merits of design, project appearance, quality and safety programs of the contractor, references, and schedule.

- **Qualifications-based selection:** Otherwise known as the dog and pony show, this method is utilized when the owner chooses a contractor based on qualifications alone. I see this done in municipal and quasi-government work all the time, and I highly discourage it. Unless you are operating under some type of cost-plus, open book contractual arrangement, you are setting yourself up for cost overruns. The selection process for this method includes issuing an RFP and reviewing responses under the following suggested categories: contractor's experience, quality control plan, project team experience, and proposed schedule.

Payment Vehicles

- **Lump sum:** Most utilized in today's market, the CM or GC and the owner agree upfront on the overall cost of the project, based on the bid plans and specs, and the owner is responsible for paying that amount. The contractor is responsible for cost overruns, as long as the requirement was shown in the drawings and specs. On the flipside, the contractor can keep any additional profit generated through accelerating the schedule or finding other ways to reduce the project cost without sacrificing the required level of quality. It is important to have someone who represents your interests conduct regular inspections during the construction of a lump-sum project to ensure that you get what you pay for.

- **Cost Plus:** Under this arrangement, the owner pays the contractor for actual cost plus a pre-negotiated fee. This contract transfers the cost-overrun risk from the contractor to the owner, as any additional costs will be paid for, even if unexpected, by the owner. The contractor must be transparent under this contracting arrangement and provide access to all job cost information, as that is the basis for monthly billing and contractor fees.

- **Guaranteed maximum price (GMP):** This contract is typically used under a CM relationship as a cap or stopgap measure for a cost-plus contract. It is the same as the cost-plus contract with one exception—there is a set price that the contract will not exceed. Anything over that amount is at the contractor's or CM's risk.

- **Unit Price:** Owners use this type of contract when quantities for a specific scope of work cannot be determined in advance of bidding the project. One example would be import of fill dirt to a site where an unknown quantity of unsuitable material must be removed. The contractor is unlikely to take on the risk of an unknown quantity, and you could agree to a unit price.

Contract Items to Know for Your Protection

- **Liquidated Damages (LDs)**—LDs provide a financial penalty to the contractor for exceeding a guaranteed delivery time on a project schedule. Typically, the amount is enough to cover the owner's cost of capital and any other costs associated with the delayed occupancy. Most contractors are reluctant to agree to LDs, but if you feel strongly about your required completion date, this can be a tool to help get you there. On the flip side, some contractors may ask for early completion bonus if they are required to agree to LDs. Usually there is a lower ratio between LDs and early completion bonus. Typically, the early completion bonus will be fifty cents per day for every one dollar of LDs.
- **Mechanic's Lien**—In most states, lien law is established to ensure that subcontractors and suppliers are paid by general contractors upon receipt of payment by the project owners. Be aware of the mechanic's lien law in your state. In many states, the owner must file a notice of commencement in the public records when a project starts, in order to provide notice to any subcontractors and

suppliers as to where to file notices to owner (NTOs). Nowadays, most companies utilize a service to manage this administrative task. Caution: if you receive an NTO for a subcontractor or supplier, take care to ensure the GC paid the sub or supplier, up through the past thirty days, prior to releasing the GCs next draw. Verify this in writing by having the GC or CM provide you lien releases from all applicable subs up through the day of the latest draw.

Stages of a Construction

Project Design

During the design stage, you would work on programming and feasibility, schematic design (bridging documents for design build), design development, and contract documents.

Conceptual design and feasibility: Your designer helps to develop your goals and objectives for the building. You will make programming decisions at this stage that will end up driving building size, MEP (mechanical, electrical, plumbing) requirements, how the space will be laid out, and who will be utilizing the space. Programming must be completed prior to beginning the actual design of the building.

- **Schematic design:** According to the American Institute of Architects (AIA), "During schematic design, an architect commonly develops study drawings, documents, or other media that illustrate the concepts of the design and include spatial relationships, scale, and form for the owner to review. Schematic design also is the research phase of the project, when zoning requirements or jurisdictional restrictions are discovered and addressed."

- **Design development (DD):** DD services take the initial design documents from the schematic phase one step further. This phase lays out mechanical, electrical, plumbing, structural, and architectural details. The result is drawings that often specify design elements such as material types and the location of windows and doors. The level of detail provided in DD is determined by the owner's request and the project requirements. The DD phase often ends with a formal contract documents, the final drawings and specifications of the construction project. They are used by contractors to develop subcontracting bids, and suppliers use them for the construction process.

- **Construction Drawing (CD):** The next phase is construction documents, the CDs. Once the owner and architect are satisfied with the documents produced during DD, the architect moves forward and produces drawings with greater detail. CDs typically include specifications for construction details and materials. The level of detail in CDs may vary depending on the owner's preference. Once CDs are satisfactorily produced, the architect sends them to contractors for pricing or bidding, if part of the contract. If the CD set is not 100 percent complete, this is noted when the CDs are sent out for bid. This phase results in the contractors' final estimate of project costs.

Bid Stage

The first step of this phase is preparation of the bid documents that will go out to potential contractors for pricing. The bid document set often includes an advertisement for bids, instructions to bidders, the bid form, bid documents, the owner-contractor agreement, labor and material payment bond, and any other sections necessary for price bids. If a project has unique aspects or complex requirements, the architect and owner may elect to have a pre-bid meeting for potential contractors.

After bid sets are distributed and returned, the owner, with the help of the architect, evaluates and selects the winning bid. Any negotiation with the bidder over price or project scope, if necessary, should be done before the construction contract is signed.

The final step is to award the contract to the selected bidder with a formal letter of intent to allow construction to begin. The final deliverable is a construction contract. Once this document is signed, project construction can begin.[iv]

Pre-construction

After the contract is signed, you will provide your contractor with a notice to proceed, which gives the contractor permission to begin work on the project.

- **Construction Lien Law:** Check with your attorney to ensure you file proper notices in the public records. If your contractor fails to pay a subcontractor or one of the suppliers, you could end up paying twice for the same work.
  - Many states have variations in construction lien law.
  - In the State of Florida, it is important that the owner file a Notice of Commencement within ninety days of starting a project.
  - At this point, you should request a list of the subcontractors and suppliers on the job.
  - Each time you are ready to pay a draw, usually in thirty-day increments, you should require signed and notarized Conditional Lien Releases for each subcontractor or supplier on the project. This will provide you, the owner, with proof that subs or suppliers have been paid up through the last date you paid your contractor, ensuring that your project will not be liened due to non-payment.
- **Project Team Assignment:** Your contractor will assign a project team, which usually includes the following personnel:
  - **Project manager:** The project manager is responsible for the entire project from start to finish and should be your primary point of contact. Main priorities include schedule management, subcontract management, project coordination, and communications with inspectors, authorities, designers, and owner.

○ **Contract administrator:** The contract administrator assists the project manager as well as the superintendent with the details of the construction contract.

○ **Superintendent:** Superintendent is responsible for execution of the schedule. Where the project manager manages the strategic level of the project, the superintendent is in charge of tactical day-to-day responsibilities, including flow of materials, deliveries, and equipment. He or she is also in charge of coordinating subcontractors, construction activities, quality control, and safety on the site.

○ **Field engineer:** A field engineer is responsible for paperwork supporting the superintendent. Generally, the field engineer is responsible for shop drawing approval and managing RFIs with the design team, and also assists by monitoring quality and safety on the project site.

Procurement

The procurement stage is when the labor, materials, and equipment needed to complete the project are 'bought out' by the contractor. It is said that this is when the GC makes his money. In a lump sum or GMP contract, the contractor has already agreed to deliver the project at a specified price. Every penny saved in subcontractor and material costs during the buyout is another penny to their bottom line. Purchase order issuance is also part of the procurement stage. The project team must accelerate procurement in order to begin shop-drawing reviews and mobilize to the site to begin construction.

Construction

The construction stage begins with a pre-construction meeting, which is brought together by the superintendent. The purpose of the pre-construction meeting is to coordinate jobsite logistics, scheduling, and quality control program requirements with the subs and supplier. The next step is to mobilize to the construction site, set up required utilities and the job trailer, and build the job.

Contractor Progress Payment Schedule

A contractor progress payment schedule is a schedule of when (according to project milestones or specified dates) contractors and suppliers will be paid for the current progress of installed work. Progress payments are partial payments for work completed during a specified period, usually every thirty days, during the construction period. Progress payments are made to general contractors, subcontractors, and suppliers as the construction project progresses. Typically, an owner will hold back ten percent of a construction contract to ensure the project is closed out and is delivered in accordance with plans and specs in the required timeframe. Once the project is completed to the owner's satisfaction, all subs and suppliers have been paid, and the contractor has signed a final release, then and only then should the owner release the retainage.

Project Completion and Owner Occupancy

Once a final inspection is completed by the certifying agency, a certificate of occupancy (CO) is issued and the owner moves into the building. It is at this point that the warranty period begins; the industry standard is one year for most systems. Some systems, such as roofs, weather sealing, and HVAC systems, can go out beyond ten and twenty years. You should walk the facility with your CM, if you have one, and designer, looking at every crack and crevice. This is your last chance to identify and fix any problems that don't belong to you. Remember, once you occupy, you own it!

Key Takeaways:

Decision Points

▷ Need to decide whether to hire GC or CM

- If CM, then
  - CM Agency
  - CM at Risk

▷ Need to decide project development method

- Design-Build
- Design-Bid-Build
- CM at Risk

Look closely at the experience and past performance of the team that will be working on your project, not just the track record of the firm.

PART 2: DISPOSITION

Chapter 11:
Disposition Strategy

"Don't be afraid to give up the good
to go for the great."—JOHN D. ROCKEFELLER

Sales Process

As you have probably learned, selling commercial industrial property is generally a more complex process than selling residential property. Buyers of commercial properties are more sophisticated and have a completely different set of goals and motivating factors than buyers of residential homes. Commercial real estate, for most buyers, is all about business strategy and economics, whereas residential housing buyers tend to be more concerned with the emotions of living in the home. When it comes to business, it is important to view the process as objectively as possibly, to help avoid costly financial mistakes that can be associated with emotional buying and selling.

The sales process for industrial properties should leverage creative marketing talents in developing your marketing strategy yet also require a detailed plan of attack with military-style execution. You need to understand the value and appeal of your property as compared to the competing alternatives, and ensure your marketing message reaches every potential user in your universe of potential buyers. Investors and users are interested in the numbers, and a professional marketing package becomes critical in presenting your property in the best light possible. While each property is unique and requires its own tailored disposition strategy and marketing plan, the general process follows these steps:

1. **Perform needs analysis**—Whether you perform this exercise yourself or work with a commercial real estate advisor in the process, it is crucial to perform a needs analysis for your company. The first step in selling a building is to understand the strategic implications of disposition. Why are you selling? What financial and strategic impact will a sale have on your company? What is your personal financial situation? What are you trying to accomplish by selling the building? What do you plan to do with the proceeds from the sale? Will you be deferring capital gains by investing proceeds into a "like kind" 1031 exchange, or do you plan to put the cash in the bank? What are your options for mitigating tax liability with respect to timing of the closing? Are you more interested in getting a lump sum of cash at closing, or would you consider receiving monthly income, without the hassles of property management, through a NNN lease arrangement

with a tenant? How much, if any, do you presently owe on outstanding mortgages? Do any of those mortgages have a due-on-sale clause? These are some of the questions to consider in order to structure a customized sale transaction that will fit your specific needs.

2. **Property valuation: Broker Opinion of Value (BOV)**—It is important to consider that different buyers can afford to pay different amounts for the same property, depending on its intended use. For example, an opportunistic, bottom feeder type of local investor might be able to make his financial projections work on your property at $28 per square foot, while an institutional investor could afford to pay $45 based on their specific investment criteria. A user that will actually occupy the building for its primary business might be able to pay up to $60 per square foot for the same building. It's important to understand that there is a finite universe of potential buyers in each category, and it is your commercial real estate advisor's job to understand who your potential target buyers are, the best strategy to reach them, and how much they can pay for the property.

    There are three main valuation approaches to consider when developing a pricing strategy for marketing a property. While each should warrant consideration in your property valuation analysis, each situation is different. It is important to consider all three and give weight as your specific situation warrants.

a. Comparable approach: This takes into consideration recent and relevant comparable sale transactions as a basis of establishing market value. With enough supporting and relevant data, you can reasonably estimate (within a range) what the market will yield for your property.

b. Income approach: While users will lean more toward comparable pricing and replacement cost when determining what to pay for a property, investors are more interested with the current or potential income an industrial facility can generate. The investment value of a commercial building is directly tied to its net operating income, and a common benchmark for communicating what properties are trading at, relative to that income, is a CAP Rate. The CAP rate (or capitalization rate) of the building is determined by dividing the last year's net operating income by the potential sales price. So, another way to extrapolate value would be to multiply your property's NOI (or potential NOI) by the market CAP rate for similar properties in your area. CAP rates can vary based on many factors, including credit quality of the tenant supporting the underlying cash flow stream; the remaining term of the lease; the age, size, and condition of the subject facility; and supply and demand for similar types of investment properties. Average CAP rates have gone down significantly over the past several years, to what have become all-time lows in some markets (indicating that investors are willing to pay more for less ROI), as demand for quality investment alternatives has increased. Recently, we have seen "going-in" CAP rates for modern, Class A industrial space with investment grade tenant leases in core markets trade in the mid four percent range, while we could see some buildings with deferred maintenance and short remaining terms on underlying leases in secondary or tertiary markets trading well above the 12 percent range.

c. Replacement Cost: This portion of the analysis simply considers the cost of acquiring raw or redevelopment land in a given submarket and constructing a new comparable facility in that location (based on current prices). While it is generally not a driver in decision-making, it can add some color and perspective to the analysis.

3. **Sale and marketing plan**—The next step is to develop an individualized sales and marketing plan for your property. Who is your target audience? How do you intend to reach them? E-blast, direct mail, direct calls or visits? Broker open houses? Post to websites and exchanges? A combination of these strategies? You will need to develop a unique and professional marketing packet that shines, and effectively highlights the features and benefits of your property. It is critical you develop and execute a plan to get the property in front of the universe of potential buyers in a way that is compelling, attractive, and best conveys the reasons why those buyers should consider your property.

4. **Contact qualified buyers**—Once the marketing package preparation is done and your strategy is developed, your commercial real estate advisor should contact his or her database of qualified buyers. This should consist of both a rifle approach for highly qualified buyers that would be a great match, and a shotgun approach that effectively markets your property across the nation and world, utilizing all available Internet-based marketing options. It is not unusual that a buyer from out of state or in another country might purchase your building.

5. **Prequalify buyers**—Your advisor should interview all interested potential parties to ensure they have the proper background, resources, and interest to acquire and manage your industrial property. Effective prequalification will save you from wasted time by eliminating unqualified buyers.

6. **Potential buyer confidentiality agreement**—In some cases, you may wish to keep your transaction confidential. If so, have all prequalified potential buyers sign a confidentiality agreement, commonly referred to as a non-disclosure agreement (NDA).

7. **Provide property details to potential buyer**—In addition to the standard marketing collateral in the listing, provide all details of the property, including current leases, building plans, surveys, operating information, and any other information your advisors deem necessary to share at this point. The buyer now has an opportunity to review the compiled marketing package, which

will provide a more detailed understanding of the facility and the opportunity to acquire.

8. **Buyer site visit and review**—Once the potential buyer reviews the marketing materials and pertinent site information, he or she may want to schedule a site visit and walk through the building. This should typically be required of any potential buyer that is interested in submitting an offer or letter of intent (LOI).

9. **LOI and counteroffer**—Generally, the buyer's broker will draft and present a letter of intent that outlines the general terms and conditions of an offer. The LOI is non-binding and is used to agree on key terms before spending the time and resources in developing an actual purchase and sale agreement. The LOI generally includes price, terms, deposit amounts and intervals, contingencies, seller financing requests, assignability, due diligence period, and a potential closing date. Your real estate advisor will present all offers to you and assist you in analyzing the LOI. Work together with your advisor to determine if you will a) respond with a counteroffer, b) accept the LOI as is, or c) not respond to the LOI. If you respond, you will continue this process until you either reach an agreement and move to the contract phase or pass on the LOI and move on.

10. **Contract phase**—At this point, your team will develop a purchase and sale agreement that embodies the previously agreed upon terms and conditions from the LOI and counteroffer/negotiation process. While you may wish to begin the process with a

boilerplate draft as a starting point, have qualified legal counsel, one that specializes in commercial real estate transactions, review any agreement prior to executing final agreements. This could prevent costly mistakes you may regret for a long time going forward.

11. **Purchase and sale agreement management**—Once both parties execute the purchase and sale agreement, the clock starts ticking (unless some other specified effective date has been set). It is important for you or your commercial real estate advisor to develop an abstract of the agreement, with key dates, and include those dates in your calendar. An example of an abstract is shown on the following page. Missing a deliverable by a key date could end up costing you big. Both parties must perform in accordance with the agreement throughout the contract period.

12. **Due diligence**—Once the contract is signed, the buyer begins the due diligence process. Your commercial real estate advisor will facilitate the process and provide the buyer with the information he or she needs. Generally, you can expect the buyer to physically inspect the building, perform a Phase I environmental analysis (along with Phase II if necessary), obtain a survey, review title exceptions and zoning restrictions, and perform other tasks as required. (Download a sample due diligence checklist at www.warehouseveteran.com). Once the due diligence period is over, the buyer cannot back out from the deal without forfeiting the deposit (unless otherwise specified in the contract).

623-627 N. 20TH ST, LLC
SALE AGREEMENT ABSTRACT
KEY DATE LOG

Milestone	Date	Note	Status
Contract Effective Date	1/13/2015	None	Done
Buyer to Deliver Deposit	1/14/2015	$20,812.50 in Escrow	Done
Seller to deliver DD package	1/23/2015	Seller to deliver copies of data, records, and documents related to property	In Progress
Seller to deliver Title Commitment	1/23/2015	Seller to deliver title commitment	Done
Deadline to Object to Title & Survey Defects	2/2/2015	+ 10 days from receipt of title or survey defects	Done
Deadline to Obtain Current Survey	2/2/2015	Check for encroachments & title issues	Done
Seller to deliver Estoppel Letters	2/22/2015	Must object to any issues before end of inspection	Pending
End of Inspection Period	2/27/2015	Subject to resolution of estoppel issues	Pending
1st Deposit Goes Hard	2/27/2015	N/A	Pending
2nd Deposit Due	2/27/2015	N/A	Pending
2nd Deposit Goes Hard	2/27/2015	N/A	Pending
Closing Date	3/14/2015	Final Checks	Pending

13. Closing—After all contract conditions have been met, your transaction should close and funds will be distributed to the appropriate parties, in accordance with the closing statement. The title agency handling the closing should provide you and your real estate advisor with a draft closing statement at least a week prior to the closing date, so you can review it and object to any issues prior to closing. Do not wait until the last minute to review this, as it can add unnecessary stress and potentially delay the closing, which is never good for either party.

Selecting a broker

I often see property owners shooting from the hip when selecting a broker to represent them in the sales process. While most people enjoy working with people they like (me included), too often, relationship elements end up driving the selection process. Working with an advisor who listens, communicates well, and is friendly is an easy path to take. And while these are admittedly important traits when selecting a friend, likeability is not the best basis for selecting a commercial real estate advisor to sell your property. Instead, what we typically see from sophisticated clients is a selection process that consists of establishing selection criteria, conducting interviews,

> All speech is vain and empty unless it be accompanied by action.
> – Demosthenes

and making a decision based on a combination of objective scoring and the human factor of likeability.

If you have your own set of criteria in mind for the selection process, that's great. Here are some other questions and considerations to discuss in an interview or, using a more formal approach, weigh and score using a decision matrix. Again, a sample decision matrix can be downloaded at **www.warehouseveteran.com**.

Questions for Potential CRE Advisors:

- How long have you been selling and/or leasing commercial real estate?
- What product types do you specialize in (general, industrial, retail, land, etc.)?
- Do you specialize in buying, selling, leasing, or some combination of the three?
- How many transactions have you completed in your career?
- Can you provide a list of transactions for the past three to five years, with a map showing their locations?
- What sets you apart from other brokers in the industry?
- Can you give me five references from owners for whom you have sold properties in the past three years?

Proposed Marketing Plan for This Property:

- What is your proposed approach to marketing my property?

- What is your estimated value of this property and proposed pricing strategy?
- What are the characteristics of the likely buyers for this property?
- How will you reach those potential buyers?
- How long do you estimate it will take to sell the property?
- How many properties in this approximate size range have sold in the past two to three years in this sub-market?
- What is the price range and price per square foot for those properties, and how did they differ from my property?
- Who were the buyers of those properties, and what were the properties used for?

Interviewing potential advisors based on these questions should give you a sense of how to separate the top players from the bottom tier brokers. The important point here is that you should follow a selection process and consider at least two or three options before committing to a broker or team. Your decision could impact your life and financial situation in a major way. Selecting the right advisor can pay you big dividends for many years going forward, not to mention make your life easier and more enjoyable during the sales process.

Selling Considerations

Dress up your property. When preparing to sell any type of real estate, it is important to boost the visual appeal of the site and the building.

In most cases, a minimal investment will yield considerable return on investment, and may significantly reduce the marketing time required to sell. Most of us recognize this fact and understand it is much easier to extract a higher price for an asset that is visually appealing.

Make sure both the inside and outside of the building are clean and appear to be well maintained. If you don't have the capital to invest in expensive repairs, consider at least setting aside enough to spruce up the landscape, pressure wash the exterior as necessary, and clean the inside and outside thoroughly. New carpet and paint in the facility's office area delivers a strong benefit, especially if your target buyer is a user, someone who will occupy the space, rather than an investor. Either way, if prospective buyers can't see themselves in your business environment, they probably won't make an offer.

Consider prepping, sealing, and painting interior and exterior warehouse walls, if necessary. Soliciting quotes from multiple qualified painting contractors can save you big in this department, since project pipelines and contractor commitments can vary significantly from firm to firm. Remember, deferred maintenance sends a signal of the seller's investment in prior maintenance of the building and presents a potential sign of things to come for any new prospective buyer.

Tax Considerations

It is important to keep track of your cost-basis on your warehouse throughout the life of your ownership of this asset for tax purposes.

Basis is not only important in determining depreciation deductions for tax purposes. It also becomes particularly important when you sell. If not calculated properly, on a continuing basis, it could result in significantly higher capital gains taxes if you sell at a profit.

The cost-basis of your property, also called the tax basis, starts with your investment in the facility when you first acquired it. The Internal Revenue Code 26 USC 2012 states that, in calculating your basis, the purchase price of your facility—which includes your down payment and the amount of mortgage—is added to the closing costs incurred with the purchase of your facility. Closing costs are all the fees you paid as the buyer, both on and off the closing statement, in acquiring the property. These sometimes include the title search and recordation fees; legal fees; title insurance; sales, excise, and transfer taxes; abstract fees; and other fees related to the transaction. Be sure to exclude loan closing costs, property insurance, liability insurance premiums, occupancy-related services or utilities prior to closing, and refinance mortgage fees. Consult your CPA to confirm your basis in your property.

Adjustments to Basis

The basis of your warehouse will increase or decrease during your ownership due to various reasons. This will affect your tax implications, and you will need to compute and track the adjusted basis of your property periodically over the ownership period. The IRS defines adjusted basis as a property's original cost-basis after certain tax-allowed adjustments.[v] Code 26 USC 1016 states that these adjustments include costs for capital improvements that increase basis, while annual depreciation deductions decrease the basis. Your warehouse can be depreciated over a thirty-nine-year recovery period by allocating the basis between the actual land and the building, and then dividing the building's basis by thirty-nine. Your CPA should calculate the adjusted basis each year in preparing your tax return for filing.

Capital Gains/Recapture Taxes: Sales Effect

When it is time to calculate your potential capital gains from the potential sale of warehouse, you will need to know your adjusted cost-basis in your property. Your gain will be computed from the disposition of the facility by determining the amount realized from the sale minus the adjusted basis. The lower the adjusted basis on your real estate, the more capital gains tax exposure you have at the time of sale. The current long term capital gains tax is either 15 percent or 20 percent, depending on your annual income bracket.

Additionally, you need to consider the impact of depreciation re-capture taxes at the time of sale. If your warehouse sells for more than its depreciated value, which is simply the adjusted basis minus all the depreciation you claimed during ownership, you will be subject to depreciation recapture tax at a 25 percent maximum rate on the difference between the facility's depreciated value and its adjusted basis. It is important to include all tax implications when making critical disposition decisions with your industrial real estate. Your CPA, along with a good commercial real estate advisor, can assist you in modeling the effects of the various tax liabilities under different sales scenarios and arm you with the information you need to make an informed decision.

Computing Basis and 1031 Exchanges

One way to defer capital gains taxes is through utilization of a Section 1031 tax deferred exchange.[VI] Whether this is your first time using this tax deferral strategy, or if you purchased your warehouse through a Section 1031 exchange, you can defer capital gains taxes on the sale of your property through reinvesting in "like-kind" or similar real estate property. When you elect this option, the basis for your old property is carried forward to the new investment property, subject to two time limits or the benefit will be lost.

The first limit is that you have forty-five days to identify potential replacement properties from the date you sell the relinquished property. The identification must be in writing, signed by you, and delivered to a person involved in the exchange, such as the seller of the replacement property or his qualified intermediary. It is important to remember that notice to your attorney, real estate advisor, accountant, or a similar person acting as your agent is not sufficient. The replacement property or properties must be clearly described in the written identification. In the case of commercial real estate, this means a legal description, street address, or distinguishable name. Follow the IRS guidelines for the maximum number and value of properties that can be identified. See IRS Guide FS-2008-18 for detailed information.

The second time limit is that the replacement property must be received and the exchange completed no later than 180 days after the sale of the exchanged property or the due date (with extensions) of the income tax return for the tax year in which the relinquished property was sold, whichever is earlier.

Computing the basis in a 1031 exchange can be fairly complicated and must be carefully and continuously calculated by a qualified 1031 intermediary or CPA when you are close to selling your property. It is important to properly calculate your cost-basis to objectively identify and analyze all your options. Your 1031 intermediary and commercial real estate advisor will help you understand the pros and cons of all your sales options.

Sale-Leaseback Option

Most companies we work with are not primarily in the business of owning real estate, but they are utilizing industrial buildings to distribute, store, or manufacture their products. A sale-leaseback is a strategic tool that can allow your company to leverage your real estate equity as a source of financing, while still having full use of the facility in exchange for paying rent over a specified period of time.

On the flip side, a sale-leaseback provides an attractive investment option for certain investors, due to the long-term stability of income streams from these lease agreements. Over the past few years, sale-leasebacks have become increasingly popular as an alternative to structured debt financing because companies can convert real estate assets to cash without adding debt to their balance sheets.

Key Benefits to You

- In most cases, little to no change in operating control of the facility.
- You negotiate the terms of the lease, including rent, lease, and renewal terms. You can also negotiate in terms that might work to your advantage, like pre-negotiated extensions and early termination options.
- It is a simplified transaction and a short closing process, compared to the typical loan process.

- There is an opportunity to monetize 100 percent of the value of the equity in your property by selling, versus the 70 percent to 80 percent LTV that you may receive if you financed your facility.
- Your company's liquidity is improved by converting balance sheet long term asset value to cash.
- In most cases, you will be able to write off the entire lease payment as expense against earnings, thereby offering tax savings opportunities.

Benefits to the Investor

- In most cases, they are getting a strong credit tenant with low potential turnover.
- Hands-off ownership with a NNN lease.
- Residual value of the building.
- Secure, predictable, long-term cash flow.

Fundamentals of Analysis

When performing an objective financial analysis for sale-leasebacks, you are comparing three potential alternative courses of action:

1. Sell to an investor and leaseback for a specified period of time.
2. Continue to occupy the space for the same period of time under the current arrangement.

3. Continue to occupy the space for the same period of time and finance/refinance, leveraging equity in your building through available debt financing.

For purposes of simplicity, let's focus on comparing a sale-leaseback against keeping your current arrangement in place with no refinance. We can compare almost every potential option in a commercial real estate decision by determining the Net Present Value (NPV) of each alternative. By distilling the after-tax cash flow from each period through applying your firm's discount rate, we can determine the value of each investment alternative in today's dollars. Large companies typically use after-tax cost of capital as the discount rate. Smaller firms and individual investors typically utilize their opportunity cost or minimum required return as the discount rate for a given investment. This may vary, depending on the estimated level of risk.

For example, if one option is to continue to own and operate your building as is over the next seven years, and you have determined through NPV analysis that the Net Present Value is a negative $210,000, and the NPV of your sale-leaseback option would be a positive $575,000, the sale-leaseback provides the superior economic option. Of course, this analysis is purely a financial exercise and does not take other subjective and strategic factors into account. In my experience, the NPV analysis is useful to include as one of many decision criteria on your decision-making matrix.

Financial Statement Impact

Another consideration in analyzing sale-leaseback options is the potential effect the transaction may have on your financial statements. The first step is to work with your advisor to determine if your potential lease would be considered an operating lease or a capital lease. Since the two lease classifications are treated differently, for both financial statement and tax purposes, it is important to understand the implications of your specific lease classification. In most cases, you will want your lease considered as an operating lease since, very often, the operating lease provides both superior tax implications and financial statement impact. If you are uncertain about the potential impact for your company, consult both your commercial real estate advisor and your CPA. Your lease would be considered a capital lease if it meets any one of the following criteria[vii]:

- The period of the lease encompasses at least 75 percent of the remaining useful life of the facility.
- Ownership of the facility is transferred from the lessor to the lessee by the end of the lease period.
- The present value of the minimum lease payments required under the lease is at least 90 percent of the facility's fair value at the inception of the lease.
- The lessee can buy the facility from the landlord at the end of the lease term for a below-market price.

An operating lease obligation is reported in your financial statement notes as a contingent liability, compared to a capital lease being reflected on the balance sheet. Therefore, your company would achieve a lower debt-to-equity ratio, which could favorably affect your cost of debt and the equity of your core business. Additionally, your rent is entered as an expense on your income statement, reducing your corporate income tax liability. Any tenant improvements paid by your company are entered on your balance statement as an asset, less accumulated depreciation. Your Tenant Improvements (TI) depreciation is included as an expense on your income statement, straight-lined over the lease term.

Sale Leaseback Conclusion

A sale-leaseback can provide your company with excellent financing options for growth and expansion, as well as a partial exit strategy. It is attractive because there are benefits for both the buyers and the sellers. The lease could provide your company long-term control and use of the property, with a positive balance sheet impact. The lease provides the investor with conditions for an outstanding commercial real estate investment, such as a reduced vacancy risk with a long-term occupier, a stable income stream, and elimination of operating expense variation risk.

Properly structured, a sale-leaseback transaction could effectively utilize your company's real estate assets as a financing tool, though the decision should be made only after the thorough analysis and comparison of your options. Because of this, it is important to work with an experienced team of CPAs, attorneys, and commercial real estate advisors to structure a deal that best meets your requirements. If you decide you wish to pursue the sale-leaseback option, it also is important your commercial real estate advisor reaches out to the universe of qualified, special purpose investors that will provide a market price for the real estate and negotiate a market lease with your team.

Key Takeaways

- A sale-leaseback can provide your company with excellent financing options for growth and expansion, as well as a partial exit strategy.
- It is important to work with an experienced team of CPAs, attorneys, and commercial real estate advisors to structure a deal that best meets your requirements.
- Be sure you understand the value and appeal of your property as compared to the competing alternatives, and ensure your marketing message reaches every potential user in your universe of potential buyers.

Conclusion

This book started with a simple goal: To develop something meaningful, a reference guide, that would give back to the world the knowledge, research, and advice I have gathered through my own experiences over the years, as well as information gained through interviews and research on relevant industrial real estate topics. Through the process of writing, compiling, and editing this field manual, it has become so much more than a reference guide.

Over the course of the last year, *Warehouse Veteran* has connected me with so many exceptional professionals with so much to share. I have personally come out of this process having gained more than a published book. Together, with all of the book's contributors, we have developed a tool that will help prevent potential loss for those who take the time to review the concepts and help others to build additional wealth.

Warehouse Veteran is reference manual, a general guide, and a road map to set you up for success. In the very broadest sense, this book is an appeal for the reader to be strategic, to think through the possibilities and outside the box in order to build a plan and find the best way to execute that plan. In some cases, that might mean going out and recruiting a team of more experienced professionals. If you run a manufacturing, distribution, or other service company, chances are you aren't also a commercial real estate expert. Knowing when to seek advice and how to weed through to find the best advisor is a requirement for success in the information age.

Leading edge businesses focus on what they do best. Remember, thoughtful strategic planning, followed with systematic execution, produces superior results in all areas, be it wartime, peacetime, or the day-to-day business world. So, when it comes to analyzing and managing commercial real estate needs, stay informed, ask the right questions, and find the brightest and best to help you prosper! Best of Luck!

John B. Jackson, CCIM

Glossary
of General Commercial Real Estate Terms

A

Abatement: A lease term typically referred to as 'free rent,' which may occur outside or in addition to the primary term of the lease.

Absorption: The amount, usually expressed on a square foot basis, at which available space in the marketplace is leased during a predetermined period of time. Also referred to as "Market Absorption."

Absorption Rate: The net change in space available for lease between two dates, typically expressed as a percentage of the total square footage.

Ad Valorem: The term means "according to value." This is a general property tax imposed on the value of property, which is typically based on the local government's valuation of the property.

Allowance Over Building Shell: Most often used in a build-to-suit scenario, the tenant has a blank canvas upon which to customize the interior finishes to their specifications. This arrangement caps the landlord's expenditure at a fixed dollar amount over the negotiated price of the base building shell. This arrangement is most successful when both parties agree on a detailed definition of what construction is included and at what price.

Annual Percentage Rate (APR): The actual cost of borrowing money, expressed in the form of an annual interest rate. It may be higher than the note rate because it represents full disclosure of the interest rate, loan origination fees, loan discount points, and other credit costs paid to the lender.

Appraisal: An estimate of opinion and value based upon a factual analysis of a property by a qualified professional.

Appreciation: The increased value of an asset.

"As-Is" Condition: The acceptance by the tenant or buyer of the existing condition of the premises at the time the lease is consummated or the property is purchased. This would include any physical defects.

Assessment: A fee imposed on property, usually to pay for public improvements such as water, sewers, streets, improvement districts, etc.

Attorn: To turn over or transfer money or goods to another. To agree to recognize a new owner of a property and to pay him/her rent.

B

Balloon Payment: A large principal payment that typically becomes due at the conclusion of the loan term. Generally, it reflects a loan amortized over a longer period than that of the term of the loan itself (i.e. payments based on a 25-year amortization with the principal balance due at the end of five years).

Base Rent: A set amount used as a basis for minimum rent in a lease, sometimes with provisions for increasing the rent over the term of the lease.

Building Classifications: Building classifications in most markets refer to Class "A," "B," and "C" properties. While the rating assigned to a particular building is very subjective, Class "A" properties are typically newer buildings with superior construction and finish in excellent locations with easy access, attractive to credit tenants, and which offer a multitude of amenities. These buildings, of course, command the highest rental rates in their sub-market. As the "Class" of the building decreases (i.e. Class "B" or "C") one component or another such as age, location, or construction of the building becomes less desirable. Note that a Class "A" building in one sub-market might rank lower if it were located in a distinctly different sub-market just a few miles away containing a higher end product.

Building Code: The various laws set forth by a states and/or municipalities that dictate the criteria for design, materials, and type of improvements allowed.

Building Standard: A list of construction materials and finishes that represent what the Tenant Improvement (Finish) Allowance/Work Letter is designed to cover, while also serving to establish the landlord's minimum quality standards with respect to tenant finish improvements within the building. Examples of standard building items are: type and style of doors, lineal feet of partitions, type/quantity of lights, quality of floor covering, etc.

Build-out: The space improvements put in place for tenant's beneficial use per specifics usually defined in the lease agreement. Takes into consideration the amount of Tenant Improvement Allowance provided for in the lease agreement.

Build-To-Suit: An approach taken to lease space by a property owner where a new building is designed and constructed per the tenant's specifications.

C

CAM Charges: Common Area Maintenance charges are one of the net charges billed to tenants in a multi-tenant commercial triple net (NNN) lease. A CAM charge is an additional rent, charged on top of base rent, and is mainly composed of maintenance fees for work performed on the common area of a property. Each tenant pays their pro rata share of a property's total CAM charges, determined by the percentage of the tenant's rented square footage of the total, rentable square footage of the property.

Cap and Collar: A term and method used in some market review clauses. This mechanism specifies a "cap" or maximum amount by which the rent can be increased, or a "collar," the maximum the rent can decrease, on the rental rate review date. As industrial leasing markets strengthen, these review methods are more difficult to negotiate.

Capitalization: A method of determining value of real property by considering net operating income divided by a predetermined annual rate of return.

Capitalization "CAP" Rate: The rate that is commonly used as a benchmark in trading of commercial investment properties. Cap Rate = Net Operating Income / Current Market Value (sales price) of the asset. The Cap Rate shows the potential rate of return on the real estate investment. While a Cap Rate can give you an idea of the rate of return of a given investment, it is not an exhaustive measure by itself.

Carrying Charges: Costs incidental to property ownership, other than interest (i.e. taxes, insurance costs and maintenance expenses) that must be absorbed by the landlord during the initial lease-up of a building and thereafter during periods of vacancy.

Certificate of Occupancy: A document presented by a local government agency or building department certifying that a building and/or the leased premises (tenant's space) has been satisfactorily inspected and is/are in a condition suitable for occupancy.

Clear-Span Facility: Term referring to a building design condition (most commonly in a warehouse) where the vertical columns are designed on the outside edges of the structure allowing for a "clear span" with no interior columns.

Comparables: Lease rates and terms (or historical sale prices in case of a purchase) of properties similar in size, construction quality, age, use, and typically located within the same sub-market and used as comparison properties to determine the fair market lease rate (or purchase price) for another property with similar characteristics.

Concessions: Cash or cash equivalents expended by the landlord in the form of rental abatement, additional tenant improvement allowance, moving expenses, cabling expenses, or other resources expended to influence or entice the tenant to sign a lease.

Construction Management: The overall planning, coordination, and control of a construction project from beginning to completion. The process is overseen by a qualified construction manager, who ensures that the various stages of the construction process are completed in a timely and seamless fashion, from getting the construction permit to completion of the construction to the final walk-through of the completed facility.

Contiguous Space: Multiple adjacent suites/spaces within a multi-tenant facility in the same building, which can be combined and rented to a single tenant.

Contract Documents: The complete set of approved plans and specifications for the construction of a building or of a building's interior improvements. These documents are part of the contract and specify the exact manner in which a project is to be constructed.

Conveyance: Most commonly refers to the transfer of title to property between parties by deed. The term may also include most of the instruments by which an interest in real estate is created, mortgaged or assigned.

Covenant: A written agreement inserted into deeds or other legal instruments stipulating performance or non-performance of certain acts, or uses or non-use of a property and/or land.

D

Deed: A legal instrument transferring title to real property from the seller to the buyer upon the sale of such property.

Default: The general failure to perform a legal or contractual duty or to discharge an obligation when due. Some specific examples are: 1) Failure to make a payment of rent when due. 2) The breach or failure to perform any of the terms of a lease or purchase agreement.

Demising Walls: The partition wall that separates one tenant's space from another or from the building's common area, such as a public corridor.

Design/Build: A construction method where a single entity is responsible for both the design and construction of a project. The term can apply to an entire facility or to individual components of the construction to be performed by a subcontractor.

Depreciation: Spreading out the cost of a capital asset over its estimated useful life or a decrease in the usefulness, and therefore value, of real property improvements or other assets caused by deterioration or obsolescence.

E

Earnest Money: The monetary advance by a buyer of part of the purchase price to indicate the intention and ability of the buyer to carry out the contract.

Easement: A right of use over the property of another created by grant, reservation, agreement, prescription, or necessary implication. It is either for the benefit of adjoining land ("appurtenant"), such as the right to cross A to get to B., or for the benefit of a specific individual ("in gross"), such as a public utility easement.

Economic Feasibility: A building or project's feasibility in terms of costs and revenue, with excess revenue establishing the degree of viability.

Economic Rent: The market rental value of a property at a given point in time, even though the actual rent may be different.

Effective Rent: The actual rental rate to be achieved by the landlord and tenant after deducting the value of concessions from the base rental rate paid by a tenant, usually expressed as an average rate over the term of the lease.

Eminent Domain: A power of the state, municipalities, and private persons or corporations authorized to exercise functions of public character to acquire private property for public use by condemnation, in return for just compensation.

Encroachment: The intrusion of a structure which extends, without permission, over a property line, easement boundary, or building setback line.

Encumbrance: Any right to, or interest in, real property held by someone other than the owner, but which will not prevent the transfer of fee title (i.e. a claim, lien, charge or liability attached to and binding real property).

Equity: The fair market value of an asset less any outstanding indebtedness or other encumbrances.

Escalation Clause: A lease clause that provides for the rent to be increased to reflect changes in expenses paid by the landlord such as real estate taxes, operating costs, etc. This may be accomplished by several means such as fixed periodic increases, increases tied to the Consumer Price Index, or adjustments based on changes in expenses paid by the landlord in relation to an expense stop or base year reference.

Estoppel Certificate: A signed statement certifying that certain statements of fact are correct as of the date of the statement and can be relied upon by a third party, including a prospective lender or purchaser. In the context of a lease, a statement by a tenant identifying that the lease is in effect and certifying that no rent has been prepaid and that there are no known outstanding defaults by the landlord (except those specified).

Escrow Agreement: A written agreement made between the parties to a contract and an escrow agent. The escrow agreement sets forth the basic obligations of the parties, describes the monies (or other things of value) to be deposited in escrow, and instructs the escrow agent concerning the disposition of the monies deposited.

Exclusive Agency Listing: A written agreement between a real estate broker and a property owner, in which the owner promises to pay a fee or commission to the broker if specified real property is leased or sold during the listing period. The broker need not be the procuring cause of the lease.

Expense Stop: An agreed dollar amount of taxes and operating expense (expressed for the building as a whole or on a square foot basis) over which the tenant will pay its prorated share of increases. May be applied to specific expenses (e.g., property taxes or insurance).

F

Fair Market Value: The sale price at which a property would change hands between a willing buyer and willing seller, neither being under any compulsion to buy or sell and both having reasonable knowledge of the relevant facts.

Finance Charge: The amount paid for the privilege of deferring payment, including any charges payable by the purchaser as a condition of the loan.

First Generation Space: Generally refers to new space that is currently available for lease and has never before been occupied by a tenant.

First Mortgage: The senior mortgage which, by reason of its position, has priority over all junior encumbrances. The holder of the first or senior mortgage has a priority right to payment in the event of default.

First Refusal Right or Right Of First Refusal (Purchase): A lease clause giving a tenant the first opportunity to buy a property at the same price and on the same terms and conditions as those contained in a third party offer that the owner has expressed a willingness to accept.

First Refusal Right or Right Of First Refusal (Adjacent Space): A lease clause giving a tenant the first opportunity to lease additional space that might become available in a property at the same price and on the same terms and conditions as those contained in a third party offer that the owner has expressed a willingness to accept. This right is often restricted to specific areas of the building, such as adjacent suites or other suites on the same floor.

Flex Space: A building providing its occupants the flexibility in utilizing the space. Usually provides a shell with configuration options, allowing a flexible amount of office or showroom space in combination with manufacturing, laboratory, warehouse distribution, etc. Generally constructed with little or no common areas, load-bearing floors, loading dock facilities, and high ceilings.

Floor Area Ratio (FAR): The ratio of the gross square footage of a building to the land on which it is situated. Calculated by dividing the total square footage in the building by the square footage of land area.

Force Majeure: A force that cannot be controlled by the parties to a contract and prevents said parties from complying with the provisions of the contract. This includes acts of God such as a flood or a hurricane, or acts of man, such as a strike, fire, or war.

Foreclosure: A procedure by which the mortgagee (lender) either takes title to or forces the sale of the mortgagor's (borrower's) property in satisfaction of a debt.

Full Recourse: A loan on which an endorser or guarantor is liable in the event of default by the borrower.

Full Service Rent: An all-inclusive rental rate that includes operating expenses such as taxes, insurance, CAM, utilities, and maintenance for the first year. The tenant is generally still responsible for any increase in operating expenses over the base year amount.

G

General Contractor: The prime contractor who contracts for the construction of an entire building or project, rather than just a portion of the work. The general contractor hires subcontractors (e.g., plumbing, electrical, etc.), coordinates all work, and is responsible for payment to subcontractors.

Gross Absorption: A measure of the total square feet leased over a specified period of time with no consideration given to space vacated in the same geographic area during the same time period.

Gross Lease: A lease in which the tenant pays a flat sum for rent, out of which the landlord must pay all expenses such as taxes, insurance, maintenance, utilities, etc.

Ground Rent: Rent paid to the owner for use of land, normally on which to build a building. Generally, the arrangement is that of a long-term land lease (e.g. 20 - 99 years) with the lessor retaining title to the land.

Gross Effective Rent: Amount of rent payable under a lease, accounting for all incentives and including all building expenses.

Gross Face Rent: Rent payable under a lease, excluding any incentives but including all building expenses.

Guaranty: Agreement whereby the guarantor undertakes collaterally to assure satisfaction of the debt of another or perform the obligation of another if and when the debtor fails to do so. Differs from a surety agreement in that there is a separate and distinct contract rather than a joint undertaking with the principal.

H

Hard Cost: The cost of actually constructing the improvements (i.e. construction costs).

Highest and Best Use: The use of land or buildings that will bring the greatest economic return over a given time and that is physically possible, appropriately supported, and financially feasible.

Hold Over Tenant: A tenant retaining possession of the leased premises after the expiration of a lease.

I

Improvements: In the context of leasing, the term typically refers to the alterations made to or inside a building, but it may also include any permanent structure or other development, such as a street, sidewalks, utilities, etc.

Indirect Costs: Development costs, other than material and labor costs, which are directly related to the construction of improvements, including administrative and office expenses, commissions, architectural, engineering, and financing costs.

J

Judgment: The final decision of a court resolving a dispute and determining the rights and obligations of the parties. Money judgments, when recorded, become a lien on real property of the defendant.

Judgment Lien: An encumbrance that arises by law when a judgment for the recovery of money attaches to the debtor's real estate.

L

Landlord's Lien or Warrant: A warrant from a landlord to levy upon a tenant's personal property (e.g., furniture, etc.) and sell it at a public sale to compel payment of the rent or the observance of some other stipulation in the lease.

Lease: An agreement whereby the owner of real property (i.e., landlord/lessor) gives the right of possession to another (i.e., tenant/lessee) for a specified period of time (i.e., term) and for a specified consideration (i.e., rent).

Lease Agreement: The formal legal document entered into between a landlord and a tenant to reflect the terms of the negotiations between them; that is, the lease terms have been negotiated and agreed upon, and the agreement has been reduced to writing. It constitutes the entire agreement between the parties and sets forth their basic legal rights.

Lease Commencement Date: The date usually constitutes the commencement of the term of the lease for all purposes, whether or not the tenant has actually taken possession, so long as beneficial occupancy is possible. In reality, there could be other agreements, such as an Early Occupancy Agreement, which have an impact on this strict definition.

Lease-Up Period: That period of time, following construction of a new building, when tenants are actively being sought and the project is approaching its stabilized occupancy.

Leasehold Improvements: Improvements made to the leased premises by or for a tenant. Generally, especially in new space, part of the negotiations will include, in some detail, the improvements to be made in the leased premises by the landlord.

Legal Description: A geographical description identifying a parcel of land by government survey, metes and bounds, or lot numbers of a recorded plat, including a description of any portion thereof that is subject to an easement or reservation.

Legal Owner: The term is in technical contrast to equitable owner. The legal owner has title to the property, although the title may actually carry no rights to the property other than as a lien.

Letter Of Attornment: A letter from the grantor to a tenant, stating that a property has been sold, and directing rent to be paid to the grantee (buyer).

Letter Of Credit: A commitment by a bank or other person, made at the request of a customer, that the issuer will honor drafts or other demands for payment upon full compliance with the conditions specified in the letter of credit. Letters of credit are often used in place of cash deposited with the landlord in satisfying the security deposit provisions of a lease.

Letter Of Intent: A preliminary agreement stating the proposed terms for a final contract. They can be "binding" or "non-binding." This is the threshold issue in most litigation concerning letters of intent. The parties should always consult their respective legal counsel before signing any Letter of Intent.

Lien: A claim or encumbrance against property used to secure a debt, charge, or the performance of some act. Includes liens acquired by contract or by operation of law. Note that all liens are encumbrances, but all encumbrances are not liens.

Lien Waiver (Waiver of Liens): A waiver of mechanic's lien rights, signed by a general contractor and his subcontractors, that is often required before the general contractor can receive a draw under the payment provisions of a construction contract. May also be required before the owner can receive a draw on a construction loan.

Like-Kind Property: A term used in an exchange of property held for productive use in a trade or business or for investment. Unless cash is received, the tax consequences of the exchange are postponed pursuant to Section 1031 of the Internal Revenue Code.

Listing Agreement: An agreement between the owner of a property and a real estate broker, giving the broker the authorization to attempt to sell or lease the property at a certain price and terms in return for a commission, set fee, or other form of compensation.

Lot: Generally, one of several contiguous parcels of land making up a fractional part or subdivision of a block, the boundaries of which are shown on recorded maps and "plats."

Lump-Sum Contract: A type of construction contract requiring the general contractor to complete a building or project for a fixed cost, normally established by competitive bidding. The contractor absorbs any loss or retains any profit.

M

Market Rent: The rental income that a property would command on the open market with a landlord and a tenant ready and willing to consummate a lease in the ordinary course of business; indicated by the rents landlords were willing to accept and tenants were willing to pay in recent lease transactions for comparable space.

Market Study: A forecast of future demand for a certain type of real estate project that includes an estimate of the square footage that can be absorbed and the rents that can be charged.

Marketable Title: A title that is free from encumbrances and could be readily marketed (i.e., sold) to a reasonably intelligent purchaser who is well informed of the facts and willing to accept such title while exercising ordinary business prudence.

Market Value: The highest price a property would command in a competitive and open market under all conditions requisite to a fair sale with the buyer and seller, each acting prudently and knowledgeably in the ordinary course of trade.

Mechanic's Lien: A claim created by state statutes for the purpose of securing priority of payment of the price and value of work performed and materials furnished in constructing, repairing, or improving a building or other structure, and which attaches to the land as well as to the buildings and improvements thereon.

Mortgage: A written instrument creating an interest in real estate and that provides security for the performance of a duty or the payment of a debt. The borrower (i.e., mortgagor) retains possession and use of the property.

N

Net Absorption: The square feet leased in a specific geographic area over a fixed period-of-time after deducting space vacated in the same area during the same period.

Net Lease: A lease in which there is a provision for the tenant to pay, in addition to rent, certain costs associated with the operation of the property. These costs may include property taxes, insurance, repairs, utilities, and maintenance. There are also "NN" (double net) and "NNN" (triple net) leases. The difference between the three is the degree to which the tenant is responsible for additional costs.

Non-Recourse Loan: A loan that bars a lender from seeking a deficiency judgment against a borrower in the event of default. The borrower is not personally liable if the value of the collateral for the loan falls below the amount required to repay the loan.

Normal Wear and Tear: The deterioration or loss in value caused by the tenant's normal and reasonable use. In many leases, the tenant is not responsible for "normal wear and tear."

O

Open Space: An unimproved area of land or water, or containing only such improvements as are appropriate to the use and enjoyment of the open area, and dedicated for public or private use or enjoyment or for the use and enjoyment of owners and occupants of land adjoining or neighboring such open spaces.

Operating Cost Escalation: Although there are many variations of escalation clauses, all are intended to adjust rents by reference to external standards such as published indexes or expenses related to the owner-ship and operation of buildings. The intent is to ensure that the escalations in operating costs do not erode income from base rental rates over the term of the lease.

Operating Expenses: The actual costs associated with operating a property including maintenance, repairs, management, utilities, taxes, and insurance. A landlord's definition of operating expenses is likely to be quite broad, covering most aspects of operating the building, which will vary by market, property, and the individual owner's approach.

P

Parking Ratio: The intent of this ratio is to provide a uniform method of expressing the amount of parking available at a given building. Dividing the total rentable square footage of a building by the building's total number of parking spaces provides the amount of rentable square feet per each individual parking space (expressed as 1/xxx or 1 per xxx). Dividing 1000 by the previous result provides the ratio of parking spaces available per each 1000 rentable square feet (expressed as x per 1000).

Pass Throughs: Refers to the tenant's pro rata share of operating expenses (i.e. taxes, utilities, repairs) paid in addition to the base rent.

Performance Bond: A surety bond posted by a contractor guaranteeing full performance of a contract with the proceeds to be used to complete the contract or compensate for the owner's loss in the event of nonperformance.

Preleased: Refers to space in a proposed building that has been leased before the start of construction or in advance of the issuance of a Certificate of Occupancy.

Prime Tenant: The major tenant in a building, or the major or anchor tenant in a shopping center serving to attract other, smaller tenants into adjacent space because of the customer traffic generated.

Pro rata: Proportionately; according to measure, interest, or liability. In the case of a tenant, the proportionate share of expenses for the maintenance and operation of the property.

Punch List: An itemized list, typically prepared by the architect or construction manager, documenting incomplete or unsatisfactory items after the contractor has notified the owner that the tenant space is substantially complete.

Q

Quitclaim Deed: A deed operating as a release intended to pass any title, interest, or claim that the grantor may have in the property, but not containing any warranty or professing that such title is valid.

R

Raw Land: Unimproved land that remains in its natural state.

Raw Space: Unimproved "shell space" in a building.

REO (Real Estate Owned): Real estate that has come to be owned by a lender, including real estate taken to satisfy a debt. Includes real estate acquired by lenders through foreclosure, or in settlement of some other obligation.

Real Property: Land, and generally whatever is erected or affixed to the land, such as buildings and fences, and including light fixtures, plumbing and heating fixtures, or other items which would be personal property if not attached.

Recourse: The right of a lender, in the event of a default by the borrower, to recover against the personal assets of a party who is secondarily liable for the debt (e.g. endorser or guarantor).

Rehab: An extensive renovation of a building or project which is intended to cure obsolescence of such building or project.

Renewal Option: A clause giving a tenant the right to extend the term of a lease, usually for a stated period of time, and at a rent amount as provided for in the option language within a predefined period.

Rent: Compensation or fee paid, usually periodically (i.e. monthly rent payments), for the occupancy and use of any rental property, land, buildings, equipment, etc.

Rent Commencement Date: The date on which a tenant begins paying rent. The dynamics of a marketplace will dictate whether this date coincides with the lease commencement date or if it commences months later (i.e., in a weak market, the tenant may be granted several months free rent). It will never begin before the lease commencement date.

Rental Concession: Incentive a landlord may offer a tenant in order to secure their tenancy. Rental abatement is one form of a concession, and there are many others including: increased tenant improvement allowance, signage, lower than market rental rates, and moving allowances.

Representation Agreement: An agreement between the owner of a property and a real estate broker giving the broker the authorization to attempt to sell or lease the property at a certain price and terms in return for a commission, set fee, or other form of compensation.

Request for Proposal ("RFP"): The formalized Request for Proposal represents a request for compilation of basic economic and business terms related to property acquisition and should be customized to reflect the tenant's specific needs. Just as the building's standard form lease document represents the landlord's "wish list," the RFP serves in that same capacity for the tenant.

S

Sale-Leaseback: An arrangement by which the owner occupant of a property agrees to sell all or part of the property to an investor and then lease it back and continue to occupy space as a tenant. Although the lease technically follows the sale, both will have been agreed to as part of the same transaction.

Second Mortgage: A mortgage on property that ranks below a first mortgage in priority. Properties may have two, three, or more mortgages, deeds of trust, or land contracts as liens at the same time. Legal sequence priority, indicated by the date of recording, determines the designation first, second, third, etc.

Second Generation or Secondary Space: Refers to previously occupied space that becomes available for lease, either directly from the landlord or as sublease space.

Security Deposit: A deposit of money by a tenant to a landlord to secure performance of a lease. This deposit can also take the form of a Letter of Credit or other financial instrument.

Setback: The distance from a curb, property line, or other reference point, within which building is prohibited.

Setback Ordinance: Setback requirements are normally provided for by ordinances or building codes. Provisions of a zoning ordinance regulate the distance from the lot line to the point where improvements may be constructed.

Shell Space: The interior condition of the tenant's usable square footage when it is without improvements or finishes. While existing improvements and finishes can be removed, thus returning space in an older building to its "shell" condition, the term most commonly refers to the condition of the usable square footage after completion of the building's "shell" construction but prior to the build out of the tenant's space. Shell construction typically denotes the floor, windows, walls, and roof of an enclosed premises and may include some HVAC, electrical, or plumbing improvements, but not demising walls or interior space partitioning.

Site Analysis: The study of a specific parcel of land, which takes into account the surrounding area and is meant to determine its suitability for a specific use or purpose.

Site Development: The installation of all necessary improvements (i.e. installment of utilities, grading, etc.) made to a site before a building or project can be constructed upon such site.

Site Plan: A detailed plan that depicts the location of improvements on a parcel of land and also contains all the information required by the zoning ordinance.

Soft Cost: That portion of an equity investment other than the actual cost of the improvements themselves (i.e. architectural and engineering fees, commissions, etc.) that may be tax-deductible in the first year.

Space Plan: A graphic representation of a tenant's space requirements, showing wall and door locations, room sizes, and sometimes furniture layouts. A preliminary space plan will be prepared for a prospective tenant at any number of different properties, and this serves as a "test-fit" to help the tenant determine which property will best meet its requirements. When the tenant has selected a building of choice, a final space plan is prepared, which speaks to all of the landlord and tenant objectives and is then approved by both parties. It must be sufficiently detailed to allow an accurate estimate of the construction costs. This final space plan will often become an exhibit to any lease negotiated between the parties.

Specific Performance: A requirement compelling one of the parties to perform or carry out the provisions of a contract into which he has entered.

Speculative Space: Any tenant space that has not been leased before the start of construction on a new building.

Subcontractor: A contractor working under and being paid by the general contractor. Often a specialist in nature, such as an electrical contractor, cement contractor, etc.

Subdivision Plat: A detailed drawing depicting the manner in which a parcel of land has been divided into two or more lots. It contains engineering considerations and other information required by the local authority.

Subordination Agreement: As used in a lease, the tenant generally accepts the leased premises subject to any recorded mortgage or deed of trust lien and all existing recorded restrictions, and the landlord is often given the power to subordinate the tenant's interest to any first mortgage or deed of trust lien subsequently placed upon the leased premises.

Surety: One who, at the request of another, and for the purpose of securing to him a benefit, voluntarily binds himself to be obligated for the debt or obligation of another. Although the term includes guarantor and the terms are commonly, though mistakenly, used interchangeably, surety differs from guarantor in a variety of respects.

Surface Rights: A right or easement granted with mineral rights, enabling the possessor of the mineral rights to drill or mine through the surface.

Survey: The process by which a parcel of land is measured and its boundaries and contents ascertained.

T

Tax Base: The assessed valuation of all the real property that lies within the jurisdiction of a taxing authority, which is then multiplied by the tax rate or mill levy to determine the amount of tax due.

Tax Lien: A statutory lien, existing in favor of the state or municipality, for nonpayment of property taxes. It attaches only to the property upon which the taxes are unpaid.

Tax roll: A list or record containing the descriptions of all land parcels located within the county, as well as the names of the owners or those receiving the tax bill, assessed values, and tax amounts.

Tenant (Lessee): One who rents real estate from another and holds an estate by virtue of a lease.

Tenant At Will: One who holds possession of premises by permission of the owner or landlord, the characteristics of which are an uncertain duration (i.e. without a fixed term) and the right of either party to terminate on proper notice.

Tenant Improvements: Improvements made to the leased premises by or for a tenant. Generally, especially in new space, part of the negotiations will include, in some detail, the improvements to be made in the leased premises by the landlord.

Tenant Improvement ("TI") Allowance: Defines the fixed amount of money contributed by the landlord toward tenant improvements. The tenant pays any of the costs that exceed this amount.

Title: The means whereby the owner of lands has the just and full possession of real property.

Title Insurance: A policy issued by a title company after searching the title, which insures against loss resulting from defects of title to a specifically described parcel of real property, or from the enforcement of liens existing against it at the time the title policy is issued.

Title Search: A review of all recorded documents affecting a specific piece of property to determine the present condition of title.

Trade Fixtures: Personal property that is attached to a structure (i.e. the walls of the leased premises) and used in the business. Since this property is part of the business and not deemed to be part of the real estate, it is typically removable upon lease termination.

Triple Net (NNN) Rent: A lease in which the tenant pays, in addition to rent, certain costs associated with a leased property, which may include property taxes, insurance premiums, repairs, utilities, and maintenances. There are also "Net Leases" and "NN" (double net) leases, depending upon the degree to which the tenant is responsible for operating costs.

Turn Key Project: The construction of a project in which a third party, usually a developer or general contractor, is responsible for the total completion of a building (including construction and interior design), or the construction of tenant improvements to the customized requirements and specifications of a future owner or tenant.

U

Under Construction: When construction has started but the Certificate of Occupancy has not yet been issued.

Under Contract: A property for which the seller has accepted the buyer's offer to purchase is referred to as being "under contract." Generally, the prospective buyer is given a certain period of time in which to perform its due diligence and finalize financing arrangements. During the period of time the property is under contract, the seller is precluded from entertaining offers from other buyers.

Unencumbered: Describes title to property that is free of liens and any other encumbrances. Free and clear.

Unimproved Land: Most commonly refers to land without improvements or buildings, but it can also mean land in its natural state. See also, "Raw Land."

Use: The specific purpose for which a parcel of land or a building is intended to be used or for which it has been designed or arranged.

V

Vacancy Factor: The amount of gross revenue that pro forma income statements anticipate will be lost because of vacancies, often expressed as a percentage of the total rentable square footage available in a building or project.

Vacancy Rate: The total amount of available space compared to the total inventory of space and expressed as a percentage. This is calculated by multiplying the vacant space times 100 and then dividing it by the total inventory.

Vacant Space: Refers to existing tenant space currently being marketed for lease. This excludes space available for sublease.

Variance: Refers to permission allowing a property owner to depart from the literal requirements of a zoning ordinance that, because of special circumstances, causes a unique hardship. Included would be such things as the particular physical surroundings, the shape or topographical condition of the property, and when compliance would result in a practical difficulty and would deprive the owner of the reasonable use of the property.

W

Working Drawings: The set of plans for a building or project that comprise the contract documents and indicate the precise manner in which a project is to be built. This set of plans includes a set of specifications for the building or project.

Z

Zoning Ordinance: Refers to the set of laws and regulations, generally at the city or county level, controlling the use of land and construction of improvements in a given area or zone.

Acknowledgements

The development of Warehouse Veteran is the culmination of efforts from many trusted friends and advisors. First and foremost, a major thank you to my beautiful wife Melanie, who stands by my side and relentlessly pushed me to 'finish the book' when it wasn't always convenient for me to lock myself in a room or go to a local coffee shop for an entire Saturday. She is an inspiration, my biggest supporter, and my best friend.

I am also thankful for the tremendous amount of support I have received from Colliers International. Colliers is a global leader in commercial real estate services, and I am proud to be associated with the professional men and women who run the enterprise.

A debt of gratitude to my business partner and mentor, Jan Boltres. Jan is a top-notch professional and has always been there to lend a hand, share experiences, and offer support.

Our market leader, Ryan Kratz. I have come to realize that Ryan is what we refer to in the military as a "leader who serves". Humble in his approach, extremely knowledgeable and effective, I give thanks to Ryan for his support and role in making Warehouse Veteran a reality.

To my mentor, Colonel C. David Poche. Although no longer with us, the experiences and lessons that Colonel Poche shared made a lasting impact on my life as a military officer, a leader, and citizen of our great country. Loved by many and always respected for his stern, witty demeanor, Colonel Poche always joked that 'if hearing the national anthem didn't make the hair on your neck stand up, you must be a communist.'

To my mentor, Ron K. Bailey. They say that dads come in many different forms, but you don't have to be a biological father to have a direct and meaningful impact on someone's life. Thank you for your friendship and support. Your direct, objective advice has always been spot-on and extremely helpful in helping me navigate through the various risks and opportunities that business presents.

To my mom and dad, thank you for your unyielding support and guidance over the years.

I would also like to give special thanks to all of the experts featured in the book for their contributions and sage advice including: Craig Robinson, Lee Arnold, Dwight Hotchkiss, Jack Rosenberg, Lee Morris, Bill Robey, John Dunphy, Dale Ingle, and Ed Miller.

And of course, last but not least, the person who kept the train on the tracks and enabled me to complete this journey, my project manager and editor, Karen Rowe.

About the Author

Deploying to Desert Storm at the age of 19, John had an early introduction to strategic planning and execution in the real-world situations found in the deserts of Iraq. As a long term business owner, commercial real estate investor, and advisor, John is passionate about sharing the lessons he's learned with anyone who could benefit from hearing of his past successes and challenges.

With a rare and diverse background as a developer, licensed site and underground utility contractor, licensed General Contractor, Fortune 100 financial analyst, and real estate consultant, John's unique perspective on commercial real estate is unmatched in the industry.

John's direct experience as an owner, buyer, seller, landlord, and tenant of commercial properties arms him with the 360 degree insight he needs to be a powerful and effective strategic advisor on the commercial real estate battlefield.

He is strategic, driven, and downright aggressive at developing and executing the plan.

All Proceeds Donated to Veterans Causes

One hundred percent of the proceeds from this book will be donated to veteran-related causes such as the Intrepid Fallen Heroes Fund, Paws for Patriots, and the Fisher House Foundation. Every dollar you and others spend on purchasing this book and all related materials will go directly to fund veterans' charitable organizations.